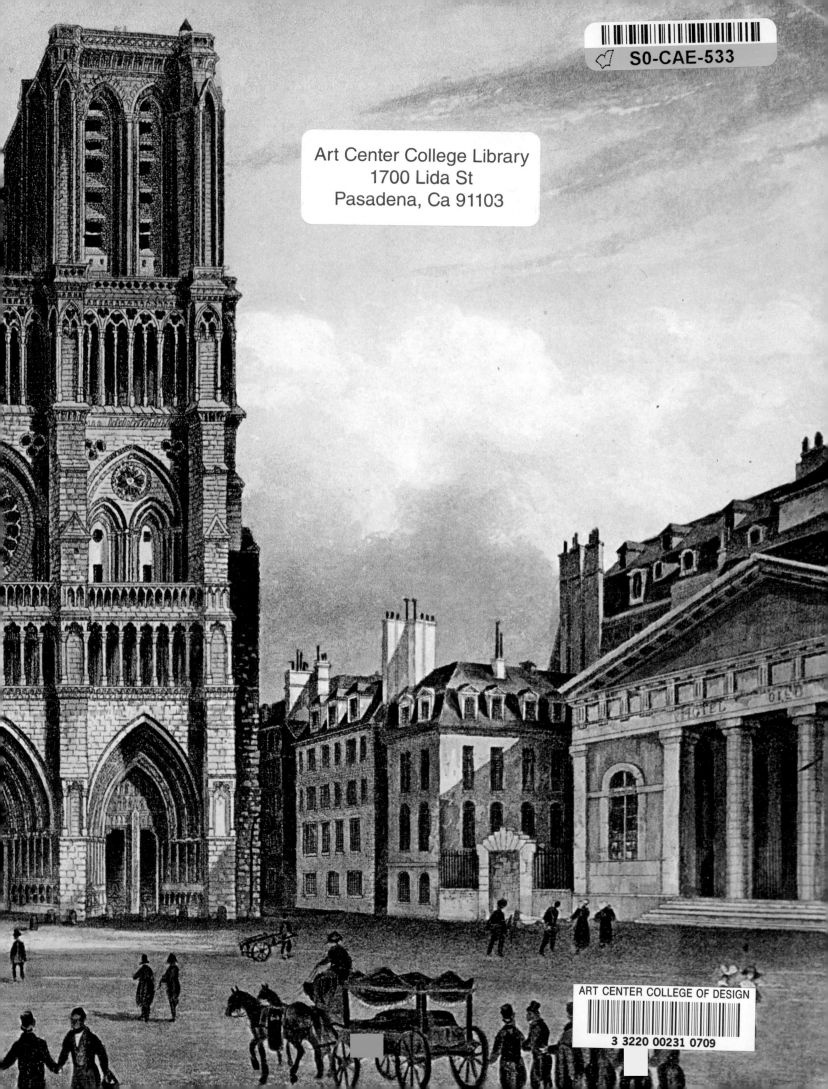

WONDERS OF MAN

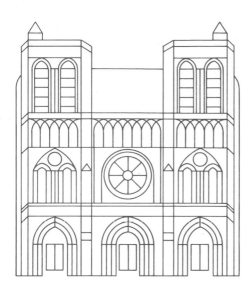

NOTRE-DAME
DE PARIS

by Richard and Clara Winston

and the Editors
of the Newsweek Book Division

NEWSWEEK, New York

NEWSWEEK BOOK DIVISION

JOSEPH L. GARDNER   *Editor*

Janet Czarnetzki   *Art Director*
Edwin D. Bayrd, Jr.   *Associate Editor*
Laurie P. Phillips   *Picture Editor*
Eva Galan   *Assistant Editor*
Lynne H. Brown   *Copy Editor*
Russell Ash   *European Correspondent*

S. ARTHUR DEMBNER   *Publisher*

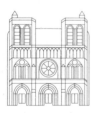

WONDERS OF MAN

MILTON GENDEL   *Consulting Editor*

Library of Congress Catalog Card No. 73-154727
© 1971—Arnoldo Mondadori Editore, S.p.A.
All rights reserved. Printed and bound in Italy.

Contents

A silver and gilded copper reliquary known as the right arm of Saint Louis, the thirteenth-century King of France.

A nineteenth-century plan by Viollet-le-Duc shows Notre-Dame's western façade as it might have looked with the spires originally intended to crown the towers.

Introduction

The "aged queen of French cathedrals," Victor Hugo called Notre-Dame de Paris in 1831. And to the famous novelist, the historic church was indeed ancient: nearly seven hundred years had passed since Bishop Maurice de Sully decided that the capital of France needed a cathedral worthy of its emerging preeminence. "Every face, every stone of the venerable monument," continued Hugo, "is a page not only of the history of the country, but also of the history of science and art." For this reason, the authors of the following narrative have selected Notre-Dame — neither the oldest, the largest, nor even the most beautiful Gothic cathedral — as the stage on which to present their dramatic review of a millennium of French history.

It was at Notre-Dame that the Crusades were preached, Te Deums sung for victories, funerals conducted for the noble and royal dead. Mary Queen of Scots was married there, Napoleon crowned, Joan of Arc beatified. Charles de Gaulle came to the cathedral to celebrate the liberation of Paris from the Nazis in 1944, and twenty-six years later the great of the world assembled to mourn the passing of France's man of the mid-century. Far more than a house of worship, the cathedral of Paris has stood at the very center of French and indeed all European history since the age of faith in which it was erected.

Two hundred years in the building, Notre-Dame was never really completed according to the scheme of its original designers. By the fifteenth century the cathedral was already considered outdated; to men of the dawning Renaissance it was but a grotesque symbol of the barbarian past, a hulking, gloomy pile to which the epithet "Gothic" was contemptuously affixed. Later, baroque additions would destroy much of the original harmony, all in the name of modernization. By the time of Hugo, it took a good deal of imagination and perhaps self-deception to appreciate the grandeur of the abused shrine.

Then, an inspired and dedicated architect of the mid-nineteenth century, Eugène Emmanuel Viollet-le-Duc, began the painstaking work of restoration; and only in the present decade, with the cleansing of all Parisian monuments, has the cathedral been revealed in its pristine elegance. To reverent believers, students of history, even idly curious tourists, Notre-Dame de Paris is now, more than ever, the supremely beautiful sight in what is widely regarded as the world's supremely beautiful city.

THE EDITORS

pilgrimages and going on crusades had likewise seized him. If it seems incredible that a primitive economy and social structure could sustain these varied enterprises — perhaps the time has come to revise our notions of how primitive the organization of medieval life was.

The wealth that was poured into the making of Notre-Dame de Paris derived from two sources: the position of Paris as the seat of a steadily growing royal power, as the residence of the Capetian kings who had replaced the Carolingian line toward the end of the tenth century; and the natural fertility of the Île-de-France.

Île-de-France sounds strange to the modern ear. But in the Middle Ages regions largely surrounded by rivers were regarded as islands. The exact territory comprising the Île-de-France fluctuated with political changes; but in the broad sense it was the area surrounded by the Seine, the Oise, the Aisne, the Ourcq, and the Marne. On the whole it was a level land of deep soil, wide marshes, broad fertile plains, and dense forests. Surprisingly large remnants of those forests still stand today in the green belts surrounding Paris. The slow-flowing, navigable rivers made transport easy even before Julius Caesar came, saw, conquered, and built his straight Roman roads. Here was country predestined by geography to become a center of civilization. And the great beds of granite and limestone dispersed among the low hills of the region assured ample supplies of building materials as soon as the inhabitants should outgrow huts of wattle and daub.

Caesar's lieutenant Labienus found the Gallic tribes called Parisii established in a small settlement on an island in the Seine: the true island that is now called the Île de la Cité. To the Roman eye, the military im-

portance of the place was self-evident, and Labienus promptly began the first of the many sieges of Paris. The Gauls burned their wooden bridges to the mainland, but Roman technology made light of rivers. Labienus succeeded in crossing the Seine twice during the campaign. He easily routed the undisciplined Gauls — and the history of the Roman city of Lutetia began. The Romans fixed their permanent camp on the Left Bank, quarried stone from Mount Lutetia — as Mont-Sainte-Geneviève was then called — and in the course of the centuries of the Pax Romana provided a theater, an amphitheater, an aqueduct, baths, temples, and other public buildings. Remains of the ancient Roman *thermae* can still be seen in the Cluny Museum, which has incorporated the ruins of these baths into its structure.

Roman expansion of the city to the Left Bank did not detract from the importance of the Île de la Cité. There, protected in a later era by a Roman wall, stood the palace of the prefect, the law court, and the temple of Jupiter. It was only natural that the Romans should build this temple to the chief of their gods at the eastern end of the island. For the spot was already hallowed by a Druid shrine. With a similar impulse, the Christians erected their first basilica where Jove's altar had been overthrown. Sanctity persists, though the names of the gods change. Notre-Dame stands upon ground that has been sacred from remote antiquity.

In 1711 workmen engaged in digging a burial vault for the archbishops of Paris came upon the remains of the Gallo-Roman wall some six feet below the pavement. They also found nine blocks of stone bearing inscriptions and reliefs. These have been identified as

parts of a votive pier erected in Roman times. The finds now stand, appropriately enough, within the somewhat funereal solemnity of the Roman baths in Cluny Museum. One of the stones bears an inscription indicating that it was dedicated in the reign of the Emperor Tiberius (A.D. 14–37) by the shipowners of Paris. It is interesting to note that seventy-odd years after Caesar's conquest these wealthy native guildsmen proudly ignore the Roman name of Lutetia and refer to themselves as *nautae Parisiaci,* Parisian shipmen. The name of the city survived the Roman intrusion, just as the guild survived the vicissitudes of history for more than a thousand years.

The carving on the Roman stones, much blurred by time and long burial in the earth, is in a style that can best be described as "provincial classic." The gods in man's image — Jupiter, Vulcan, and the Gallic Esus (a Celtic parallel to Hercules) — are sculpted conventionally. More skill and passion seem to have been lavished on the fourth side of one stone, where a bull and three cranes are represented — creatures associated with the ancient cult of the Great Mother, which preceded the worship of male gods. Thus early in the history of the Île de la Cité the goddess in one of her many guises had her devotees.

The Romans were tolerant. They recognized the general identity, despite many local variations, of the great body of mythology and ritual that stretched from the mountains of Hindustan to the shores of the Atlantic Ocean. Hence they readily adopted barbarian gods, including them within their own pantheon or allowing the "natives" to continue worshiping them. If the Gauls chose to call Hercules Esus, that was their affair, so long as they paid their taxes with regularity and obeyed the laws of their Roman governors.

But when a religion claimed exclusiveness and universality, as did that of the Christians, Roman tolerance reached its limits. Persecution followed; the preachers of the new religion were crucified, thrown to lions, roasted on gridirons, broken on the rack, and beheaded. But the Romans discovered to their dismay that a faith founded on a martyrdom was only nourished by the blood of martyrs. Christianity spread. It reached from the slave quarters to the highest ranks of Roman society; and eventually, early in the fourth century, the Emperor Constantine conquered in the sign of the cross. But long before that official acceptance, Gaul had been proselytized. By the third century Christian worship was being practiced in the catacombs of Paris, and during the brief reign of the Emperor Decius (249–251) the first Bishop of Paris was tortured and executed. His name was Dionysius or, to give it the French form, Denis.

Virtually no historical facts are known about Saint Denis, but legend has been all the more active on his behalf. With his companions, Rusticus and Eleutherius, he preached the Gospel incessantly, making countless converts, until the patience of the Romans wore thin. They must in fact have been exceedingly patient, for he continued to evangelize until the age of ninety, when he was put under arrest. Despite ferocious tortures, Saint Denis refused to deny his faith. Finally he was taken to the temple of Mars and Mercury on Montmartre and there beheaded. Whereupon, according to the *Golden Legend,* "the body of Saynte Denys reysed hymselfe up and bare his hede beetwene his armes,

as the angels ledde hym two leghes fro the place which is sayd the hille of the martyrs unto the place where he now resteth by his election and the purveance of god. And there was heard so grete and swete a melodye of angels that many that herd it byleuyd in oure lorde."

The spot where Saint Denis was tortured, on the eastern end of the Île de la Cité, ultimately became a pilgrimage station and the site of a priory called Saint-Denis-du-Pas. For the religion the bishop had preached continued its conquering course unchecked by the invasion of the German tribe of Franks, who subsequently gave the country its name. Their fierce and treacherous warrior-king Clovis, who in the fifth century founded the French monarchy by murdering his neighbors, converted to Christianity under the pressure of policy and the persuasions of his wife, Clotilda. He made Paris his capital, founded the church of Sainte-Geneviève, and established a dynasty that lasted until the middle of the eighth century. Under his descendants, the city of Paris throve. Many of these Merovingians — as they were called after a possibly mythical ancestor of Clovis — proved to be as bloodthirsty as the founder of the kingdom. But some of them were cultivated, and all of them were pious. They followed Clovis's example in becoming benefactors of the Church.

By the latter part of the sixth century at least two large churches, and probably several smaller ones, stood on the Île de la Cité. Together, the two chief churches constituted the cathedral — which meant the episcopal church where the bishop had his seat, or *cathedra*. One was dedicated to the first Christian martyr, Saint Stephen; the other was already called the church of Our Lady: Notre-Dame. French archaeologists and his-

The thirteenth-century illumination at left depicts a memorable event in the history of France and Christianity — the baptism in 496 of Clovis, pagan conqueror of Gaul. Attended by bishops and noblemen, the King of the Franks submits modestly to the ritual bath of purification.

torians have recently discovered how extremely common was the practice of building two separate con-cathedrals (as well as a separate baptistery) during the so-called Dark Ages. The necessity for this practice arose out of the nature of early Christianity as a mystery religion. Large numbers of new converts were attached to the Church but had not yet received baptism. In fact, since baptism washed away all sins, a prudent believer often postponed it throughout his life. Like the Emperor Constantine, many believers were baptized only on their deathbeds — when there was little likelihood that they could commit new sins. Until baptism, the convert was known as a catechumen, a Greek word meaning "one who is under instruction."

Early Christian liturgy, which is still preserved in the liturgy of the Eastern Orthodox Church, was divided into two parts, one for the catechumens and one for the baptized believers. After the sermon and prayer, and before Consecration, the order was given: "Catechumens, go out!" Only after the catechumens had all left and the initiates were among themselves would the secret Creed be recited and the communion bread and wine be distributed.

The architecture of churches reflected this division. The narthex, usually a colonnaded porch in front of the nave of a basilica, was originally built so that catechumens could participate in the first part of the service and then depart without disturbing the rest of the congregation. But as conversions increased and Christianity spread, the narthex alone proved inadequate. It became the practice to build two separate churches: one for the initiates and one for the unbaptized faithful. Such "double cathedrals" have been iden-

tified throughout France and deep into northern Italy. Like so many similar pairs, the two on the Île de la Cité were dedicated to Saint Stephen and to the Virgin. North of these churches of Saint-Etienne and Notre-Dame there stood, from the fourth century on, the episcopal baptistery of Saint-Jean-le-Rond.

Little remains of these two early — but surely not earliest — churches on the Île de la Cité. Their foundations lie beneath or have become part of the substructures of later Merovingian churches found under the pavement and the parvis of Notre-Dame in the course of Viollet-le-Duc's excavations and reconstruction work during the nineteenth century. The walls must have been enormously thick, composed of pebbles and rough-cut quarry stones held together by cement. A form of coursing was achieved by alternating layers of flat bricks taken from ruined buildings of Roman times. These walls were plastered and painted in floral and foliage designs, red against a white background.

The Merovingian churches of Saint-Etienne and Notre-Dame were by no means small, although they would be dwarfed by the present cathedral. From the evidence of the foundations, Merovingian Saint-Etienne must have been about 170 feet long and perhaps 70 feet wide. This compares favorably with the basilica of Tours, built over the tomb of Saint Martin, which according to Gregory of Tours was 160 feet long, 60 feet wide, and 45 feet high. Undoubtedly, Saint-Etienne would have had a timbered roof, the great beams painted in brilliant colors — for the Franks loved deep reds, blues, and golds. The floor was bright with mosaic, the columns of black and white marble. Probably this marble had been lifted from older Roman ruins. The abstract painted motifs against the white plaster walls must have shown up brilliantly in the light of many windows. For the Merovingians brought as much light as possible into their churches — Gregory of Tours mentions that the basilica built over the tomb of Saint Martin was illuminated by no less than fifty-two windows and eight doors.

With the rise of the practice of infant baptism and the conversion of entire peoples to Christianity, the distinction between catechumens and the baptized had fallen into oblivion. The original reason for the existence of the two separate churches disappeared. It seems likely, though our sources are vague on the question, that the smaller church of Notre Dame continued to be associated with the inner circle of initiates and thus remained more properly the site of the bishop's *cathedra*. But Saint Étienne was more capacious. The Bishop of Paris functioned there when he wished to perform some important ceremony before a great concourse of people. Nevertheless, a feeling seems to have lingered among the Parisians that the church of Notre-Dame was the bishop's true seat.

That feeling triumphed after the disasters of the ninth century, for it coincided with the increasing fervor for the Virgin throughout the Western world. But for a time during that turbulent ninth century it seemed as if neither Christian civilization nor any Christian churches in France would survive the onslaught of the pagan Northmen. The broad, navigable rivers of France were like an open invitation to these fierce sea rovers, who were then entering upon their great period of expansion. The dragon-prowed Viking ships were the best in the world at the time, equally at home on the wild wastes of the mid-Atlantic and the tranquil rivers of Europe.

Beginning in 841, the Northmen repeatedly swept up those rivers, looting, burning, imposing tribute. Few dared oppose them. The very sight of the black ships inspired terror. France, weakened by fratricidal wars among the descendants of Charlemagne, could not put up effective resistance. Monks huddled in their walled monasteries praying, "Deliver us from the fury of the Northmen." A contemporary wrote: "And so among us the sword of barbarian men rages, unsheathed from the scabbard of the Lord! And we, wretched creatures, live as though paralyzed, not only among the hideous evils done by savages, but as well among the wars fought without pity between our own peoples, amid sedition and fraud."

Bishops, abbots, counts, dukes, and kings all paid heavy tribute to persuade the invaders to withdraw or to ransom important prisoners. But after a brief respite the pirates would always return, demanding still more silver and gold. By the middle of the century the Vikings had ravaged Poitiers, Tours, Blois, Orléans, Bayeux, Beauvais, Chartres, and many lesser places. Paris, too, was not spared. One hundred twenty Viking ships under a Danish chief named Ragnar Lodbrok sailed up the Seine in 845. King Charles the Bald awaited them with an army where the river makes a great loop to the north outside the city — for he was determined to protect his royal abbey of Saint-Denis. But his soldiers fled in terror when the Northmen callously hanged a band of captives to trees outside the walls of Saint-Denis. Then, not bothering to lay siege to the abbey this time, the Vikings moved on to Paris

and captured the city on Easter Eve. It was a mournful Easter for the Parisians. The enemy looted the monasteries and churches, slew monks and priests, and agreed to withdraw only when Charles paid them seven thousand pounds of silver.

Eleven years later another band of Vikings appeared on the Seine. On December 28, 856, Paris fell once more, and this time the churches were burned. Only Saint-Etienne, Saint-Denis-du-Pas, and Saint-Germain-des-Prés were spared — on payment of enormous bribes. Notre-Dame was evidently badly damaged, but it was probably not wholly destroyed; the Northmen were too busy looting and taking slaves to waste their time breaking down massive stone walls.

In spite of grievous sufferings and losses, the citizens of Paris were still wealthy — the monk Abbo complains of their pride, their love of purple and gold garments, and their belts studded with gems. He also reproaches them for their devotion to "the foul charms of Venus." Nevertheless, the Parisians were also devoted to the Virgin. They set to work simultaneously strengthening the defenses of their city and rebuilding Notre-Dame. In hopes of protection from pirates, they dedicated their city to Mary — a sign of the rising cult of the Virgin that was to dominate later centuries. Evidently, they performed prodigies of labor. By 868 they had sufficiently completed the work on the new cathedral to transfer to it the relics that had formerly been housed in the aging church of Saint-Etienne. One of the most precious of these relics was a nail from the True Cross, presented to Charlemagne by the Patriarch of Jerusalem sixty-nine years earlier.

Thereafter, Saint-Etienne, which had probably also

suffered some damage from the Vikings, gradually lost its status as con-cathedral. The bishop's seat stayed in Notre-Dame. Unfortunately, we have no contemporary descriptions of this rebuilt cathedral of Notre-Dame, and not a stone remains to tell us what it looked like.

The Parisians had acted with rare courage in building even while the Northmen were returning again and again to attack the city. They displayed equal courage in defense, for after the pillaging of 856 Paris did not fall again. Toward the end of the century it withstood a four-year siege, and by its heroic resistance saved the rest of France from Viking conquest.

The region around the mouth of the Seine was beyond saving. The Northmen had entrenched themselves too solidly there; and since there was little left to rob where so many of them had passed, they settled down to make use of the true wealth of the region, the land itself. Early in the tenth century Charles the Simple made the best of a bad bargain by granting to Rollo the Northman what he already held: the territory at the estuary of the Seine. In return, Rollo agreed to live at peace with the French, become the vassal of Charles, and accept Christianity.

Thus Rollo the Raider became Duke of Normandy, and the wild Northmen turned into the shrewd, hard-headed, commercial-minded Normans. Within a century they had abandoned Old Norse for the language of the people they ruled. And they ruled well. While they proved troublesome as vassals of the King of France, often growing more powerful than their overlord, they gave Normandy better government than could be found in most parts of Europe. The French-speaking Normans remained as bellicose and enterprising as their forebears; but they had learned to value permanent possession rather than piracy. In the next two centuries they more than doubled the size of their original grant in Normandy. And on their foreign adventures, they tried to hold what they seized.

These dukes of Normandy were a rough lot, domineering, treacherous, and ruthless. But in the eyes of their contemporaries they more than made up for these qualities by their piety. They adopted the Christian religion of their subjects with the zeal of converts. And although they had a reputation for being closefisted, they were always generous in their benefactions to the Church. Moreover, they threw their influence into the struggle for religious reform, which began at about the same time that they settled in Normandy. The traditional date for the cession of Normandy to Rollo is 911; the monastery of Cluny, which became the great focus of the monastic revival, was founded in 910.

In those troubled times the monasteries offered employment and security, a measure of peace in this world, and salvation in the next. No wonder men flocked to them. The new monastic orders, in particular the Cluniac and Cistercian, expanded at a fantastic pace. Each monastery needed at least a chapel; the great ones aspired to churches of a size that rivaled or exceeded the cathedrals of the cities. Well endowed by the dukes and their vassals, receiving the revenues from tracts of rich land scattered all over France and England, garnering additional wealth from their own labors in restoring wasteland to productivity, the monks had the means to build. And they built.

They were sharing the passion of the age. It is true that in many places throughout Europe older churches

Fire was an omnipresent danger to the wooden churches of the early Middle Ages. At right, monks and villagers form a fire brigade to extinguish the flames that threaten to engulf a sanctum dedicated to the Virgin.

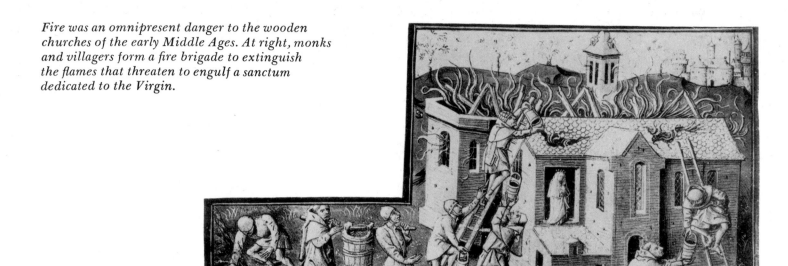

had been damaged or destroyed by the raids of Vikings, Saracens, and Magyars. But as we have seen from the example of Notre-Dame in Paris, these were quickly rebuilt, even before the invaders had been beaten back or converted. With more stable times, however, came something else: a new impulse of hope, a desire to glorify God in the works of man. Contemporaries were conscious of this new spirit. The chronicler Raoul Glaber, writing of the period after 1030, put it into famous words:

All over the world, and especially in Italy and France, people began to rebuild their churches. Most of these were well constructed and in no need of alterations. But all Christian countries were rivaling each other to see which should have the most beautiful temples. It seemed as if the world was shaking itself and casting off its old rags, was putting on here, there, and everywhere the pure white robe of churches.

In Normandy, many of the great new temples were abbey churches: Mont-Saint-Michel, Fécamp, Saint-Ouen at Rouen, Saint-Etienne and La Trinité at Caen. But the secular clergy could not long lag behind the monastics, and at Coutances, Bayeux, and Evreux the bishops likewise began building on a scale unprecedented in the history of Christian Europe. This fever for building was accompanied by an outburst of architectural creativity, by endless experimentation, ever-growing sophistication, and a passionate absorption in both the engineering techniques and the artistic expressiveness of construction. The scale of building activity rapidly produced a large corps of professional, highly skilled architects who traveled from place to place, often accompanied by itinerant masons and car-

penters. In effect, the demand created something not too different from the modern construction company.

The new architectural style that resulted from unceasing experimentation during the eleventh and twelfth centuries is known as Romanesque. The term itself was invented by a Norman archaeologist and originally applied to the whole architecture between Roman times and medieval Gothic. In the sense that the word means "like Roman," it is a misnomer; but then "Gothic" is likewise a misnomer, for Gothic art had nothing to do with the Goths. It suffices that both words by now have the sanction of tradition.

The cruciform shape of the Romanesque churches passed on into the Gothic. There is the long nave crossed toward the eastern end by a transept and terminated by the rounded apse inherited from the Roman basilica. Some Romanesque churches provided an apse on the west as well as one on the east; and quite often, as at Vézelay, there is a huge narthex, although the original reason for this covered porch had long since disappeared.

Romanesque's characteristic two towers of the western façade, and the use of sculpture around doors and arcades, were also to be perpetuated in the later Gothic churches. So also, above all, was the use of stone vaulting to close in the nave, in place of the wooden ceilings that had previously spanned the void. The narrower side aisles had been vaulted in stone earlier, but stone vaulting over the great naves represented an act of daring on the part of the builders, and it was testimony to their increasing skill and confidence.

The earliest vaults were semicircular barrel vaults, which gave a tunnel-like and rather monotonous look to a long nave. Erecting such vaults likewise required large amounts of scaffolding and centering (wooden arch supports) during construction. A device at once aesthetic and practical solved this difficulty. At regular intervals the builders introduced what are called transverse arches, running across beneath the barrel vault from pier to pier. The banded effect of the transverse arches relieved the monotony, and at the same time simplified construction; for the scaffolding could be shifted from bay to bay after each transverse arch and its accompanying section of vaulting had been placed.

As the skills of the masons advanced, dressed stone replaced the rubble and mortar used in the earliest Romanesque churches. The easily cut limestone of Normandy and the Île-de-France facilitated this practice. At the same time experimentation in vaulting continued. Over square bays, barrel vaults intersecting at right angles were tried again for the first time since Roman days. Some masons learned to strengthen these "groined vaults" by ribs along the groins, that is, at the lines where the two vaults met. A significant step toward the Gothic vault had been taken.

It has often been said that the stone vaulting that characterizes Romanesque architecture sprang from the desire to build fireproof churches — after so many Merovingian and Carolingian basilicas had been damaged or destroyed by fire during the barbarian raids of the ninth and tenth centuries. But this practical argument seems rather faulty, since wood continued to be used in the tie beams, struts, and rafters that supported the roofs over the vaulting. Moreover, since the roofs were invariably built before the vaulting, many years passed — during which the church was often in contin-uous use — before the all-stone interior was achieved. And fires continued to ravage stone-vaulted Romanesque churches after the barbarian raids had ceased. Vézelay, Chartres, Reims, Amiens, Beauvais, Canterbury — to name only some of the most famous cathedrals — suffered serious fires in the eleventh and twelfth centuries. In fact, the contemporary description of the burning of Canterbury cathedral in 1174 suggests that vaulted churches may have been subject to greater fire hazards than were earlier churches. At Canterbury sparks from burning cottages outside the gates of the cathedral were carried by the wind between the joints of the lead sheets that covered the roof. There they smoldered undetected until the whole roof was ablaze and the great tie beams came crashing down into the choir, setting fire to the monks' wooden seats. No one had noticed smoke because the fire burned so long between the elaborately painted vaulted ceiling and the roof above it.

It is more likely that the stone vaulting of the Romanesque church sprang from aesthetic and religious impulses rather than practical needs. It bespoke an ambition to build on a more magnificent scale than hitherto, a desire for glorious earthly works to express the glory of God. That spirit accompanied the upsurge in economic and political life, the rapid growth of towns and monastic orders, the increase in population, the widening of horizons that came with the Crusades, and the new concentrations of power in the Capetian dynasty in France, the Norman and Angevin dynasties in Normandy and England, the Hohenstaufen dynasty in Germany and Italy. The same spirit continued on into the Gothic era. As Frederick Artz has succinctly put it in *The Mind of the Middle Ages:* "Like the great monuments of later Roman and Byzantine architecture, huge Romanesque and Gothic churches seem built not to the measure of man and this world, but to the measure of infinity and eternity."

The origin of Romanesque architecture is a vexing question. Certainly, influences from as far east as Armenia played some part in its development. The Norman conquest of Sicily, which coincided with the Norman conquest of England, added a dynamic element to the existing Arab and Byzantine cultures of southern Italy. A century after the Norman invasion of Sicily, the cross-fertilization of Byzantine, Arab, and Norman cultures would produce the marvelous cathedral of Monreale, with its Arab apse, Byzantine mosaics, Norman capitals, and North Italian bronze doors. The skills of Greek and Arab laborers, combined with the wealth and energy of the Norman king, made this great Romanesque cathedral the product of a single impulse. Begun ten years after Notre-Dame de Paris, it was completed within the incredibly short span of eight years — while the cathedral of Paris was two hundred years in the building.

But for all that the Romanesque led the way to the Gothic, and for all the many resemblances, there is no mistaking the two styles. The Romanesque system of vaulting influenced the whole appearance of the church, and everything else flowed from that: the massiveness, solidity, dimness, the sense of power and earthbound foursquareness.

The barrel vault exerts a continuous lateral thrust along its whole length. It therefore required thick walls pierced by few openings to sustain this outward pressure. With a beamed ceiling, the thrust had been directly downward. In addition, wood is far less heavy than stone. Hence it had been easier for the builders of Merovingian and Carolingian churches to leave large openings in the walls for windows. Romanesque vaulting introduced a new harmony, consistency, and grandeur by its use of stone throughout the interior; but the churches were dark. This "dim religious light" also corresponded with the intentions of the builders; it coincided with the growing mystical spirit of the tenth to the twelfth centuries. But in the more optimistic and worldly times of the late twelfth and thirteenth centuries, when travel and the Crusades had opened so many windows on the world, builders regarded the darkness as a defect. The history of the Gothic may in a sense be regarded as an architectural striving to recapture the light that had been lost in the previous centuries. In the second quarter of the twelfth century that striving was put directly into words and stone by Abbot Suger of Saint-Denis.

II The Cathedral Crusade

For half a millennium the abbey of Saint-Denis had enjoyed the patronage of the Frankish kings. They had bestowed upon it vineyards, orchards, town and country estates, villages, forests, until it became the wealthiest abbey in France. When their royal progresses took them to the vicinity of Paris, the kings stayed at the abbey rather than in the city. And most of them made arrangements for their mortal remains to be laid to rest at Saint-Denis. "Mother of churches and crown of the realm," contemporaries called it. The abbey's prestige bothered the bishops of nearby Paris, but there seemed very little they could do about it.

One of the worst thorns in the side of the bishops of Paris, spiritual heads of a great city dedicated to commerce, was the Fair of Saint-Denis. Founded by the Merovingian ruler Dagobert I in the seventh century, the fair was held annually in October and lasted for a full four weeks. Here Venetian, Syrian, and Jewish merchants chaffered with Gascons, Lombards, Saxons, and Greeks, exchanging English wool and fleeces, Flemish cloth and hides, for silks, spices, pearls, and perfumes. And the monks of Saint-Denis reaped a handsome profit from renting booths.

For four hundred years the fair, which also drew throngs of pilgrims to the relics of Saint-Denis, proved to be an admirable source of revenue. It was so profitable that in the middle of the eleventh century the monks sought and obtained permission from King Henry I to establish an additional fair and religious feast during the summer. This became the famous Lendit, which specialized in cloth, leather, parchment, fur, and horses. The bishops of Paris eyed its success jealously; and in 1109, taking advantage of a temporary

coolness between the king and Abbot Adam of Saint-Denis, they persuaded Louis VI, the Fat, to allow them to establish a second Lendit in honor of a fragment of the True Cross that had recently been acquired by Notre-Dame de Paris. The question of the two Lendits made one more chapter in the five-hundred-year-old rivalry between the see of Paris and the abbey of Saint-Denis.

Saint-Denis was indignant over this "outer Lendit," as the new fair at Paris was called. When Louis's boyhood friend Suger became Abbot of Saint-Denis in 1122, he promptly used his influence to recapture sole rights to the Lendit for his abbey. In 1124 Louis revoked the privilege that Notre-Dame had enjoyed for only fifteen years. He granted Saint-Denis both the right to hold the fair and its site in the plain between Paris and the abbey. This was an outstanding victory for the new abbot. In addition to the considerable material benefits for the abbey, the new privilege strengthened the claims of Saint-Denis to religious primacy in France.

Abbot Suger, one of the most remarkable men in an age rich in eminent personalities, was a living demonstration that the Church was the chief avenue of social mobility in the twelfth century. The gifted son of poor parents, probably peasants, he was born around 1082. Sent to the abbey for education at the age of ten, he was thrown in with Prince Louis, the future King of France, who was attending the abbey school at the same time. Louis and Suger became fast friends for life.

Suger grew to maturity in a Church throbbing with excitement and racked by dissension over the reformist movement of Pope Gregory VII, which was carried

into the monasteries by Suger's contemporary Bernard of Clairvaux. Throughout Suger's boyhood, every pilgrim had brought stirring news of the gathering armies of the First Crusade. When he was barely seventeen, his heart leaped at the good tidings that the Holy City had been recovered from the infidel. The Crusade, coming as it did in his most impressionable years, was never far from his mind. All his life he longed to take up the cross himself, but his duties and his vocation kept him at home. Instead, he embarked upon what has often been called "the cathedral crusade."

Suger took his monastic vows at the age of twenty-four, and soon distinguished himself by his intelligence, diplomacy, and capacity for work. Abbot Adam sent him on frequent missions to Rome and elsewhere on the affairs of both the abbey and the king. By the time Adam died, it was a foregone conclusion that Suger would succeed him and inherit also the Abbot of Saint-Denis's traditional role as chief adviser to the king. In that capacity, Suger quickly became the king's mainstay in domestic and foreign policy.

Suger himself relates that even while he was still a pupil in the school of Saint-Denis, he had longed to rebuild the ancient, dilapidated abbey and abbey church. The existing Carolingian church was nearly four hundred years old. In addition to its state of disrepair, the old church was too small for the crowds that thronged into it on feast days to pray before the bones of Saint Denis, Saint Rusticus, and Saint Eleutherius, a nail of the True Cross, what then passed for the Crown of Thorns (later King Louis IX, Saint Louis, would bring the "true" Crown of Thorns to Notre-Dame), and many other relics. Suger himself has

vividly described the crush of the crowd:

> Often on feast days the crowds as they moved in opposite directions . . . prevented those attempting to enter from entering and also drove out those who had already entered. . . . No one among the countless thousands of people could move a foot because of their very density; no one, because of their very congestion, could do anything but stand like a marble statue, benumbed, or as a last resort, scream. The distress of the women, however, was intolerable; squeezed by the mass of strong men as in a wine-press, they exhibited bloodless faces as in imagined death, cried out horribly as though in labor.

From the moment he took office as abbot, Suger set about reorganizing the mismanaged affairs of the abbey, increasing its revenues, and systematically setting aside part of the increase as a building fund. Suger had that breadth of knowledge, grasp of the whole, and capacity for detail which are among the characteristics of genius. Despite his humble origins, he negotiated with popes and kings on a plane of equality; but he also saw to it that his peasants obtained improved plowshares. Under his guidance, the weak French monarchy increased its power. Simultaneously, the abbey and its many possessions throve.

In Suger's mind, the fortunes of the abbey and the fortunes of France were virtually identical. He demonstrated that conviction in the literary labors of his later years, for he divided his time between writing a life of Louis VI and a history of his own administration of Saint-Denis, with special emphasis on the building of his church. Thus we are fortunate in having an account of the spiritual motives and the practical problems of

church building from the pen of a man who conceived and directed the work. Suger controlled every phase of the building, choosing the stone from the quarries, going into the forests to find the trees for the tie beams that supported the roof, consulting with his architects on questions of design and the order of construction.

There were no real precedents for the kind of church that Suger wanted to build. The Crusaders, whose tales he eagerly listened to, had returned with descriptions of the resplendent churches of Constantinople, above all Hagia Sophia with its fabulous domes. Not that Suger thought of erecting domes; that would have been too violent a break with the tradition of the churches he had seen, and the techniques would probably have been beyond the capacities of his architects. But he wanted a similar effect of height and magnificence: he wanted vast spaces so that there would be room for all, and ample light to show to best effect the gold, gems, marble, and porphyry with which he hoped to fill his new church. For Suger loved brightness, glitter, light. And out of that love, combined with the mystique of royalty, the exaltation of mystical theology, and the long history of experimentation by the builders of Romanesque cathedrals and abbey churches, a new style was born, an architecture dominated by height and light: the Gothic.

To Suger light was more than illumination. It was metaphysical being, an emanation of divinity, of all things closest to God because least material. Light was spirit, intelligence, understanding; and the more men understood, the closer they came to God — provided they had faith. *Fides quaerens intellectum,* faith is always seeking understanding, wrote Anselm of Canter-

bury, whom Suger in his youth had undoubtedly met.

The metaphysics of light was closely bound up with Saint-Denis itself. It had been elaborated by that mysterious personality known as Dionysius the Pseudo-Areopagite. This was a fifth-century Syrian philosopher who for obscure reasons pretended to be the same person as the Dionysius of Athens who is mentioned in the Scriptures as a convert and follower of Saint Paul in the first century. His books, *On the Divine Names, On the Celestial Hierarchy, On Mystic Theology,* were avidly read by such men as Suger. And at Saint-Denis it was held as an article of faith that the scriptural Dionysius, the Syrian philosopher, and the Saint Denis who had carried his head in his hands from Montmartre to the site of the abbey in the third century, were one and the same person! A former abbot of Saint-Denis who wrote a biography of Saint Denis had declared all three identical, and how could anyone be so bold as to challenge a tradition that was three hundred years old?

Peter Abelard, the great philosopher and tragic lover, did undertake to challenge the tradition. After his affair with Héloïse came to its terrible denouement — Abelard's emasculation by her uncle's henchmen — Abelard took refuge in Saint-Denis. But that brilliant and passionate man aroused dissension wherever he went. At Saint-Denis he set about proving from texts that the Syrian philosopher had not been Saint Denis, the apostle of France. Saint-Denis angrily expelled the contentious philosopher, and Abelard took refuge in a solitary hut near Troyes — where students from all over Europe came flocking to hear his provocative lectures. But that is another story.

Suger's preparations for building his church took
many years. He announced his intentions in 1125, but
did not begin construction until 1137, the year that
Louis VI died and was succeeded by Louis VII. Masons,
sculptors, glassmakers, and other craftsmen had to be
imported from Normandy and the south, or trained
on the site, for there was not much of a building tradition in the Île-de-France at that time. Moreover, and
this was the perennial problem of medieval builders,
as far as possible the old church had to continue in use
while the new one was rising. A church was as vital to
men of the twelfth century as bread and wine, and even
more vital to a community of monks. Consequently
Suger tried to preserve as much as he could of the old
Carolingian church. He left the nave intact, tore down
the western apse of the twin-apsed church, and built a
façade with three portals and two towers, like the
Abbey of Saint-Etienne at Caen. Behind the façade he
erected a three-aisled narthex, and then a new nave to
link up with the old Carolingian nave. This work proceeded with fabulous speed; it was well advanced by
1140. Then Suger abruptly stopped work on the upper
parts of the façade towers and embarked on the building of the choir. With that choir, it has been said,
Gothic architecture began.

The choir was covered by a cross-ribbed vault, and
pointed arches were used throughout — emphasizing
that verticality which we have come to associate with
the Gothic. Surrounding the choir was a double ambulatory with nine radiating chapels whose outer walls
were reduced to mere skeletons by a pair of tall windows in each. "The entire sanctuary is thus pervaded
by a wonderful and continuous light entering through

the most sacred windows," Suger wrote enthusiastically.

"Sacred windows" may give us pause unless we understand that for the first time in architectural history Suger had filled his windows completely with stained glass. Such glass was not unknown; indeed, France seems to have been the country of its origin. But we know little about its history; few fragments of early glass have survived, and before Suger's time we have only occasional records of donations of stained glass. Suger, however, was the first to install such glass on a large scale, employing it as a form of painting with light to depict sacred subjects. And for subjects he selected those scenes from Scripture that conformed with the Pseudo-Areopagite's theology. Thus Moses appeared veiled before the people of Israel as the universe is obscured from men's understanding until they are permeated by the Divine Light. "Bright is the noble edifice that is pervaded by the new light," Suger wrote — and by "new light" he meant both his stained glass and Christ.

Miracles abound in Suger's own account of the building of Saint-Denis. It was a miracle that he had found exactly the right stone at the Pontoise quarry, a miracle that the forest contained exactly the number of trees he needed for his roof, a miracle that he secured the gems he needed to ornament the huge crucifix he set up in the choir. A collection of hyacinths, sapphires, rubies, emeralds, and topazes only recently amassed by King Henry I of England found its way by devious means into Suger's hands. "We paid four hundred pounds for the lot, though they were worth much more," he wrote with unmistakable self-satisfaction. But the greatest miracle of all was the preservation of

his unfinished choir during a storm of unprecedented violence. Suger's account of it is so important because one phrase suggests that in the building of Saint-Denis he had taken a tremendous leap toward mature Gothic architecture.

The roof of the choir had been completed and the vaulting begun. One day Bishop Geoffrey of Chartres was celebrating mass in the partly finished church. (The bishop was a frequent visitor, himself engaged in rebuilding his church and therefore interested in Suger's work. In fact, he borrowed sculptors from Suger and lent the abbot some of his workmen in return.) Suddenly a violent storm arose. Houses, stone towers, and wooden bulwarks around Saint-Denis were blown down by the force of the wind. Rain descended in torrents and the wind howled ferociously. Bishop Geoffrey at the altar, looking up at what the abbot called "principal arches," saw them "miserably trembling and swaying hither and thither." Suger's account continues:

> The Bishop, alarmed by the strong vibration of these arches and the roofing, frequently extended his blessing hand in the direction of that part and urgently held toward it . . . the arm of the aged St. Simeon [a relic]; so that he escaped disaster . . . by the grace of God and the merit of the Saints. Thus the storm, while it brought calamitous ruin in many places to buildings thought to be firm, was unable to damage these isolated and newly made arches, tottering in mid-air, because it was repulsed by the power of God.

There has been some controversy over what precisely Suger meant by "principal arches." One scholar has recently suggested that the abbot was speaking of the arches of flying buttresses. But it is possible that he was

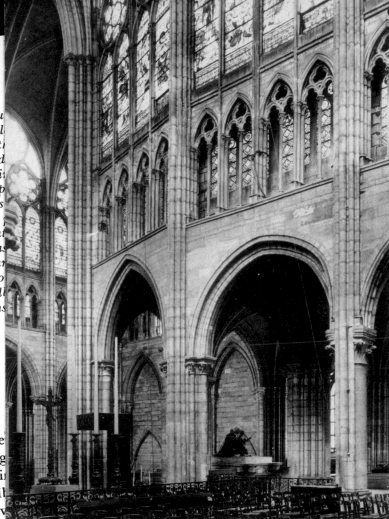

nine tie
Areopag
The Ki
the visib
in Heav
    Saint
which b
other p
praised
was tin
The ro
wanted
Denis.
return
throug
diatel
Paris
Saint
    Th
futur
of Sa
ance
Notr
have
    T
offic
for
to a
mu
bel
mo
im
lat

referring to the ribs, standing alone under the roof before the webbing had been spread between them. This would be further evidence of the way in which Gothic vaulting was constructed and a confirmation of Otto von Simson's concise verdict that Saint-Denis "was certainly the first Gothic edifice completed."

By 1144 Suger was ready for the consecration of his choir. He set the date for June 11, three days before the opening of the Lendit, so that visitors to the fair could attend. The celebration was a notable event. Young King Louis VII came with his beautiful, forceful, and newly wed queen, Eleanor of Aquitaine. The counts and nobles could not be numbered. Saint Bernard was present and Archbishop Theobald of Canterbury came from England. In all, there were nineteen bishops and archbishops simultaneously celebrating mass.

Suger's high altar glittered with gold; he had encased it in golden panels on all sides and covered it with gold as well "so that the whole altar would appear golden all the way around." For the Eucharist he had provided golden pouring vessels and golden vials. The clerics in their brilliant vestments, the royal pair and the nobles in their flashing silks, the crosses studded with gems, the many-colored light pouring down through the stained-glass windows, provided the populace with a foretaste of Heaven. And the populace was indeed represented; according to Suger himself, all of Paris came to Saint-Denis that day to see the new church and to gape at the throng of notables. With his keen sense of the theatrical, Suger arranged his bishops in two groups of nine in the choir and crypt, to correspond with the nine chapels around the choir and the

37

governing their community life were relaxed, and ultimately they became a powerful corporation of individuals with revenues of their own. Their relationship with the bishop varied widely. In some places they elected him from their own ranks; in some places they were subservient to him; in others, independent of him. The dean of a chapter was often nearly as powerful as a bishop; the chancellor was virtual secretary of the diocese; the treasurer controlled the finances of the cathedral and sometimes of the diocese as well. The chapter usually had charge of the cathedral school and was always responsible for the "fabric" — by which was meant the actual physical structure of the cathedral.

The Chapter of Notre-Dame occupied a large cloister consisting of some forty houses north of what is now the rue du Cloître Notre-Dame. It had an income of some 80,000 livres, maintained a library and a famous singing school, and was steadily growing in independence and power. In the twelfth century, however, it had not yet freed itself completely from the bishop's control, and a strong bishop could repress if not suppress the canons' taste for wine, women, a groaning board, and gambling. (In fact, not until 1335 did the long struggle come to an end when the bishop at last abandoned all claims to jurisdiction over the dean, the chapter as a body, or any of the canons as individuals.)

Maurice de Sully, like Suger of humble stock, came to Paris from Sully-sur-Loire around 1137, to study in the cathedral school. He probably heard lectures by the greatest teachers of the age, Hugh of St. Victor and Peter Abelard, and rubbed elbows with fellow students who were to be the great ecclesiastics of his own generation, John of Salisbury and Thomas Becket. Like Suger, he was the same age as his young sovereign, Louis VII, who was also educated at the cloister of Notre-Dame. Maurice soon distinguished himself by the eloquence of his preaching, the orthodoxy of his theology, and his skill in scholastic debate — venturing to oppose even the famous author of the *Sentences*, Peter Lombard. A subdeacon by 1147, Maurice rose swiftly in the hierarchy of the Chapter of Notre-Dame. In 1159 he became archdeacon shortly after none other than Peter Lombard was elected bishop.

Archdeacons were notorious in this period. As financial and administrative officers of the diocese, they were regarded as rapacious canon lawyers who lined their own sleeves (in the twelfth century men often carried money in their sleeves) by incessant exactions. "Whether an archdeacon can possibly attain salvation" was said to be a standard debating proposition in the schools. But the archdeacon also had a good chance to succeed to the episcopal seat, for the chapter tended to regard him as one of their own. If he were elected bishop, he might help his chapter for a time — until the needs of his new dignity forced him to turn to battle with his own archdeacon over revenues and prerogatives.

Maurice did not remain archdeacon long enough to imperil his salvation. Bishop Peter Lombard died in 1160. The chapter found itself unable to choose between two candidates: Maurice and Peter the Glutton, so named for his habit of devouring scholastic texts. King Louis intervened to procure the election of Maurice who, on October 12, 1160, was consecrated the seventy-fourth Bishop of Paris. Three years later, the cornerstone of Notre-Dame de Paris was laid.

Given the conditions of the time, the decision to

build a new cathedral was inevitable. Work had started on such smaller Gothic churches as Saint-Germain-des-Prés, Saint-Martin-des-Champs, and Saint-Pierre, the last at Montmartre near the supposed site of the decapitation of Saint Denis. Moreover, Paris itself had expanded mightily under the long and essentially prosperous reign of Louis VII. From the hill of Montmartre a contemporary traveler looking down upon the "turreted city surrounded by great walls" could think he was beholding Rome itself. The walls were the ancient Roman walls of the Cité, the turrets those of the Royal Palace and the Grant Chastelet, which guarded the Grant Pont. But the city had already spilled out over both banks of the Seine; a wooden palisade protected the right-bank area opposite the Île de la Cité. On this same right bank, across from what is now the Île Saint-Louis, lay the stronghold of the Knights Templar, the Temple. The Temple at this time was a financial as well as religious enterprise; it was the nearest thing to a central bank that Europe possessed. In its shadow many fine suburban houses were rising outside the stockade, for this populous city could no longer be confined within walls.

Thousands of students of many nations swarmed in the crowded streets and jammed into high-priced lodgings — sometimes as many as eighteen to a room. Vast quantities of food and wine were brought by boat up the Seine from Normandy and down the Seine from Champagne and Burgundy to be unloaded at the Chastelet and the Grève — for boats could not easily pass through the stone arches of the Grant Pont. A busy commercial mart, Paris was also a political and religious center of increasing importance. Louis VI and Louis

VII had strengthened the French monarchy, subdued rebellious vassals, and established firm ties with the papacy. Foreign dignitaries came frequently to Paris to negotiate with the king. Thomas Becket, Henry II of England, Pope Alexander III, Rainald of Dassel, simultaneously Archbishop of Cologne and Chancellor of Frederick Barbarossa's Holy Roman Empire — such eminent men acknowledged the growing importance of Capetian France by seeking the friendship of King Louis VII.

Louis himself was a pious and modest man, given to deprecating his worldly possessions. He once remarked to an Englishman: "Your master the King of England lacks nothing; he possesses men, horses, gold and silk, gems, fruits, wild beasts and all things else. We in France have nothing except bread and wine and joy." But Louis's new Bishop of Paris had more of Suger's temperament. He understood that prestige must be visible. Paris, the greatest city in France, could not lag behind such small towns as Senlis, Noyon, and Sens, and such abbeys as Saint-Denis. Paris must have a cathedral worthy of a capital.

Statues representing the king and the bishop, as well as the powerful Dean of the Chapter of Notre-Dame, can be seen to this day on the Portal of Saint Anne, the south portal of the western façade. The sculptors set to work right at the beginning of construction, carving capitals for the columns and statues for the portals — although these statues would not be inserted in their places for some forty years. The oldest part of the Portal of Saint Anne — it was rebuilt in the thirteenth century — is the tympanum, the curved triangular space under the arch. In its center the Virgin sits

Among the students who flocked to the capital in the twelfth century was Maurice de Sully, represented at right by his official seal. As Bishop of Paris, Maurice began the construction of Notre-Dame. The bas-reliefs at left from Saint Stephen's portal are thought to represent scenes from the life of Parisian scholars.

majestically on a square, ornamented throne, enclosed within turrets like a miniature cathedral. She sits with a certain hieratic stiffness, the Child on her lap, and both gaze straight ahead, as if unaware of the adoring angels to either side. Beyond the angel on her left (our right), identified by his crown and regal look, Louis VII humbly kneels. On her right Maurice de Sully asserts his ecclesiastical prerogative. He stands proudly, his crook over his right shoulder, a small and stocky man who looks more conscious of his power than does the king of his, perhaps because Maurice had traveled a longer way than Louis to achieve it.

Tucked into the corner of the tympanum to the left of Maurice, his back bowed to conform to the curve of the arch and the habit of the scribe, in his hand a book in which he seems to be making an entry, sits a man who has been identified as Barbedor, Dean of the Chapter. He is a young man with a face rather like Maurice's, except that he is beardless. Barbedor deserves his place on the façade of the cathedral. Chaplain and confessor to Louis VII, he was the direct intermediary between king and bishop. He also served for sixteen years as dean, and in that capacity supervised much of the construction. What is more, he devoted a large part of his personal wealth to furthering the work. It was he who compensated owners whose houses had to be razed and he who furnished the funds for the stained glass of the choir.

Like Suger, Maurice evidently spent the first few years of his episcopate putting his house in order, increasing revenues, accumulating a building fund, and preparing the site. A whole row of buildings on the Île de la Cité was demolished so that a new street could

be cut — the rue Neuve Notre-Dame — extending from the old church of Saint-Etienne to the highway that ran to the Petit Pont. Thus the cartloads of materials could be brought directly to the old church, which was used as a workshop. Due penance would be made for this desecration by dedicating the portal on the south façade of the new cathedral to Saint Stephen.

By that time, halfway through the third quarter of the twelfth century, so many cathedrals were rising that a vast corps of skilled workmen was available. Notre-Dame de Paris, like the other great cathedrals of the Middle Ages, was built by professional workers tightly organized in guilds, their wages established by law or by hard bargaining between the guild masters and the cathedral chapters, their practices carefully regulated by the traditions and rules of the guilds. Teams of such workmen moved from city to city, from site to site, as a particular cathedral reached the stage that called for their special skills. Contracts with these itinerant construction companies were carefully drawn up, specifying even such details as the ruling that mortarmen were to be exempt from the onerous obligation of night-watch.

Before any work could begin, the stone had to be found. Millions of tons of stone were quarried in the Île-de-France during the cathedral-building centuries — more, it has been said, than during the whole history of ancient Egypt. Fortunately, beautiful stone of varying degrees of hardness underlay much of the countryside around Paris. Most of the stone for Notre-Dame came from quarries on the Butte Saint-Jacques, from Bagneux, Arcueil, and Montrouge. The quarrymen, unlike the other workmen, tended to be residents of

the area who spent their lives amid choking clouds of stone dust. Since transportation was expensive, they cut the blocks roughly to shape in the quarry — there was little point in carting tons of waste material to the building site.

The quarryman had to know stone intimately. Working with primitive equipment, without benefit of explosives or mechanical saws, he had to find the lines of cleavage in the beds, to follow the grain of the stone. As a rule, he chose the softer varieties wherever their use would do no harm, as in the sculptures and facings. But for bearing surfaces, for the drums of columns and overhanging cornices, he had at his disposal the firm, hard stone called cliquart. No doubt the pay scales varied for the different types of stone, since the workmen were paid piecework by the block rather than by the hour.

From the quarry the stone had to be transported in oxcarts or on barges to the site. An oxcart could carry perhaps one ton — and thousands of tons of stone were needed. No wonder that the sculptors of Laon cathedral placed statues of oxen at the corners of their towers, in tribute to the patient beasts.

Sometimes men took the place of the oxen. This "cult of the carts" has given rise to the legend of whole populations rushing to aid in the work. The cult is first recorded at Chartres in 1144, when nobles and common folk harnessed themselves to the carts and dragged them to the cathedral site. Whenever they stopped to rest, they bewailed their sins, and when they arrived at Chartres they flung themselves to the ground and begged the priests to scourge them. From Chartres returning pilgrims spread the cult to Rouen and then

"Nowhere have I seen a tower like that of Laon," declared the medieval mason Villard de Honnecourt, whose whimsical sketch appears at right. The statues that perch precariously upon the towers honor the oxen whose labor helped build the great cathedrals of France.

throughout Normandy and France, wherever churches to the Virgin Mary were being built.

Such outbursts of popular enthusiasm remind us of the spirit that underlay the building of the cathedrals — a spirit that made possible the enormous financial sacrifices on the part of the common people, the clergy, and the nobles alike. But these episodes were infrequent and occurred mostly at the beginning of construction. Had they happened more often, the draymen and bargemen, who depended on the work for their daily wages, would have put a stop to such volunteer labor. Indeed, there is a story in one of the *chansons de geste* of a penitent nobleman who served in a cathedral workshop for almost nothing, out of a desire to atone for his sins. The other workmen regarded him as a scab, to use the modern term; they attacked him and beat him to death.

At the masons' lodge the stone was dressed to its final shape. The stonecutters carefully marked each block or cylinder to show where it was to be placed on the wall, column, or arch. In addition to these "position marks," they chiseled their personal marks — rarely letters of the alphabet, more often symbols: combinations of triangles, crosses, arrows, zigzag bars. These masons' marks were the equivalent of signatures; they ensured that when the week's work was totaled there would be no disputes over how many blocks each man had delivered. But the marks also served as an expression of the medieval mason's pride in his work. A father handed his mark on to his son. If a son worked on the same job with his father, he would add a small additional stroke to distinguish his own mark. By examining marks, archaeologists have been able to trace the travels of the itinerant masons from cathedral to cathedral across France.

The workshops also employed large numbers of smiths. Stone blunts iron tools swiftly, and the smiths were kept constantly busy forging or sharpening the hammers, picks, chisels, points, punches, claw chisels, drags, saws, and drills with which the masons worked. In addition, smiths made the chains that were used both for hoists and sometimes for strengthening walls and the nippers that gripped the stones — instruments rather like giant ice tongs, which were held closed by the stones' own weight. At the height of their activity the cathedral workshops were an inferno of noise: carts rumbling, masons' hammers pounding, smiths' anvils clanging, workmen shouting orders to their helpers from high up on the scaffolding or the walls.

The simplest form of stoneworking consisted of making the rough blocks that were used with rubble and mortar to fill the interior of walls and buttresses to the required thickness. Such work could safely be left to apprentices. The smoothly finished blocks of larger sizes for the facings of the cathedral — as well as the drums for the columns, the cylinders for colonnettes, the wedge-shaped voussoirs that formed the arches, and the complexly faceted keystones — required the experience and talent of the trained journeyman. The lacelike tracery of windows, the intricacies of capitals, the multiple planes and curves of moldings, were necessarily reserved for the master mason. Medieval writers did not differentiate between masons and sculptors; but it is clear that the men who carved the madonnas, patriarchs, saints, kings, and gargoyles that adorned the cathedrals knew themselves to be artists, even though they only occasionally signed their work. With the growth and spread of the Gothic style, these sculptors became more daring, more realistic, and more obtrusive. They literally covered the cathedrals with their works; there are twelve hundred sculptures in Notre-Dame de Paris, some three thousand at Reims.

The masons' lodges, originally simple workshops, in time developed into a kind of clubhouse, where the masons lived and offered hospitality to traveling members of the guild. The lodges acquired libraries of works on architecture and geometry, set up schools for teaching apprentices the mysteries of the crafts, and jealously guarded the rights of the masons.

One of the great discoveries of the medieval mason was of the extraordinary strength of a thin-shelled web with double curvature. The web is the area of a vault between the stone ribs, and in many cathedrals it is made of an extremely thin mixture of rubble stone and mortar. The ribs supported this structure during the slow setting period of medieval mortars. But it has been observed that sometimes, because of bombings or other accidents, the ribs of vaults will fall and the vaults will nevertheless hold. This fact has given rise to much controversy on the function of medieval rib-vaulting. Some writers on the Gothic have gone so far as to assert that the ribs were purely decorative. It has remained for modern builders in concrete, who rediscovered the extraordinary strength of thin curved shells — an eggshell is an example of the principle — to explain the puzzle. There is no doubt that the ribs strengthen the Gothic vault. But the effect of doubly curved, thin-shelled webbing added an extra element of strength and security. The vault webs of Notre-Dame are only six inches in thickness. Yet, they have held firm for eight hundred years!

The carpenters, of course, were as important as the masons. The lives of the workmen depended upon their care in lashing together the scaffolding poles. They built the ramps up which materials were carried and set up the shoring that held walls in position. They chose, hewed, and installed the tie beams, plates, and rafters of the roofs, binding the members together with mortise-and-tenon joints, through which wooden pegs were driven. Carpenters also had to be engineers, for they built and maintained the "great wheel," which was installed on a platform under the roof and used for hoisting stone and other heavy materials into place. These wheel-windlasses were operated by manpower, sometimes in the form of a treadmill but they afforded considerable mechanical advantage.

The greatest call upon the skills of the carpenters came in the construction of the falsework or centering, the complex curving frames that supported arches during construction. Unless the centering had the proper curvature, the stone arch would not hold when the wooden support was removed. Moreover, the process of "striking" or "decentering" called for delicate judgment. If the wooden frame was removed too soon, while the mortar was still green, the arch might collapse. But leaving the centering in place too long was also dangerous. For if the mortar had set so hard that it had lost all plasticity, when the centering was removed and the building settled, the vault might crack open. The medieval carpenters seem to have devised ingenious methods of removing wedges a little at a time, so that the arches could settle gradually as the mortar hardened. Still, it must have been a tense moment for carpenters, masons, and the master of the work alike each time the falsework was finally removed.

The master of the work, *magister operis,* sometimes called master mason or master builder, combined the roles of architect, general contractor, and chief foreman. He was on the site every day directing operations, but he also drew up the plans, made models of the projected building, organized the order of construction, and negotiated with the canons, the bishop, or the abbot. Carrying his *virga,* the measuring rod, he went about the works in elegant robes, with his gloves in his hands but not on them. These gloves were a sign that he had sprung from the guild of masons but that he now worked with his head rather than his hands.

Surviving contracts with masters of the work indicate that they were well paid and much sought after. In addition to a daily fee, they received an allowance for clothing, free food and lodging, and could eat with the monks or canons if they liked. On the other hand, they were not subject to the restrictions imposed upon monks and, sometimes, on canons. Their food allowance was one and a half times that of a monk, and on fast days they dined in the kitchen — which presumably meant that they need not keep the fast.

The masters were learned men, not untutored practical geniuses. They attended the monastic schools until they acquired a reading, writing, and speaking knowledge of Latin. Then followed years of apprenticeship to a stonemason and more years as a journeyman mason, during which they wandered over Europe studying buildings and acquiring those secrets of geometry, design, and engineering that were closely guarded in the lodges. Eventually came promotion to the honored rank of master mason. Not all master masons became workmasters, of course; only those who had genius as well as practical competence were called upon to design and build the cathedrals. Their accomplishments are the testimony to their genius. Though the word architect was seldom used in the medieval period, these men were certainly great architects.

Unfortunately, we do not know the name of the first master of the work at Notre-Dame, although a certain "Richard the mason" witnessed a cathedral document in 1164 and the names of some of the later great masters have been preserved. But it is clear, from the very fabric of the cathedral that now stands before us, that Bishop Maurice de Sully made an inspired choice. When he was ready for the laying of the cornerstone of the choir in 1163, he had at his disposal an architect whose ability matched the bishop's vision.

III — A Bible in Stone

From the point of view of Louis VII of France, the year 1163 seemed an excellent time to embark on the building of a new cathedral for his capital. Twenty-six years before, when Abbot Suger began his reconstruction of Saint-Denis, Louis had been a mere child still under the abbot's tutelage. He had just brought home his high-spirited, fifteen-year-old bride, Eleanor, heiress of Aquitaine and Poitou. On his arrival in Paris, he found his father, Louis the Fat, newly dead and himself King of the Franks at the age of seventeen. He had spent the next years in struggles with rebellious vassals, in fruitless efforts to subdue his wife, and in endless prayers to Heaven to grant him a male heir to succeed him on the throne.

Louis blamed his ill luck in fathering only daughters upon the terrible sin he had committed at Vitry on the Marne, during his war with the Count of Champagne, the most redoubtable of his vassals. Leading his army in person, Louis had set fire to Vitry. The populace had fled to the sanctuary of the church, but that too caught fire. More than a thousand men, women, and children were found burned to death in the charred ruins. For a while Louis bore the reproaches of Bernard of Clairvaux, but in the long run he could scarcely endure his own contrition. Waking and sleeping, he heard the cries of the victims, the roar of the flames. He fell into such a deep depression that for a time his physicians feared for his life.

It was partly in penance for the horror of Vitry that Louis took the cross seven years later. Abbot Suger, with many misgivings, consented to act as regent of France during the king's absence on the Second Crusade. But although Saint Bernard himself had blessed the Crusade, God in his inscrutable wisdom evidently had not. Deceived by the Byzantines, ambushed by the Turks, beset by hunger, thirst, and plague, the vast army of Franks, Flemings, Poitevins, Aquitanians, and Germans dissolved into a disorderly rabble. Franks quarreled with Germans, Louis's men with Eleanor's men; and the king and queen had their private disputes as well. Eleanor threatened divorce, and Louis had to lead her back to Europe a virtual captive.

When they reached Italy after a harrowing voyage, Pope Eugenius III tried to restore harmony to the young royal pair. He went so far as to bed them down together in his own palace, on a couch spread with brocades, and talk to them like a father to his children. But the reconciliation was brief, and three years later the pair separated for good — in those days grounds of consanguinity could always be found when politics or pique required royal divorces. Louis kept their daughters, but he had to swallow the bitter pill of returning to Eleanor her lands of Poitou and Aquitaine. The pill tasted even worse when these lands immediately fell to his most formidable rival Henry Plantagenet, the Duke of Normandy, who promptly married Eleanor. Two years later Eleanor wore a crown once more, for her new husband became King Henry II of England. Moreover, Eleanor gave Henry what she had denied Louis: a son. And more male heirs followed. A dismayed Louis could not know that Henry Plantagenet would have little joy of his sons when they were grown to manhood.

Louis hurriedly married Constance of Castile. She died in 1160, leaving him with two more daughters to add to the two he already had by Eleanor. Terrified

by the prospect of extinction of the Capetian line, Louis entered his third marriage less than a month after Constance's death. His choice fell upon Alix of Champagne; the marriage had the additional merit of settling his old quarrel with the counts of Champagne.

By 1163, when he attended the dedication of Notre-Dame cathedral, Louis's years of travail seemed over. The adroit diplomacy of Thomas Becket, Henry II's chancellor, had at last settled the intermittent war between France and England on the borders of Normandy and Aquitaine. Becket had partly reconciled the two kings and effected a marital alliance between them by betrothing Henry's son Henry to Princess Marguerite, the daughter of Louis and Constance. By then Henry of England's attention was focused on his growing quarrel with his former chancellor, for he had unwisely made Thomas Becket Archbishop of Canterbury. The new archbishop became an obstinate defender of the rights of the Church against the Crown. On the other side of Louis's kingdom, Emperor Frederick Barbarossa was engaged in a similar struggle against the Church, and he had carried it so far as to drive Pope Alexander III into exile and set up an antipope. Thus Louis, ruler of a small country hemmed in by hungry and aggressive neighbors, could for the time being breathe easier. His antagonists were preoccupied, and Louis, in the prime of life, could turn his attention to the arts of peace, which by temperament he preferred.

In a perilous middle position, France relied on her traditional religious orthodoxy. Louis therefore welcomed the exiled pope to France. The close alliance between France and the papacy went back more than four hundred years, and Louis VII, like his predeces-

sors, took pride in the epithet "most Christian King." If France could not brandish the mightiest sword in Europe, she could nevertheless lead the way in the battles of the Lord. Already Louis felt that he was winning all the campaigns in the cathedral crusade, and he gave generously to help Maurice de Sully build a church worthy of his capital city.

The king's largesse, however, could not sustain so vast a project. Funds had to be raised from every possible source. Maurice de Sully, like the other great episcopal and abbatial builders of the time, employed all the usual methods for raising money. Human vanity was exploited: the right to be buried inside the cathedral was sold before a donor's decease and even before there was a cathedral to be buried in. For the sake of a plaque testifying to their donation, the faithful gave the profits of a fishpond or a mill or a barge or a ferry. The guilds of shoemakers, fishermen, glassmakers, ironmongers, and whatnot were invited to make contributions. Appeals were repeatedly made to nobles and wealthy merchants. Maurice personally persuaded a notorious usurer to offer a large sum to the building fund in order to win remission of his sins.

But the most effective method of raising money was the dispatch of missions. A party of canons, headed by the most eloquent members of the chapter, was provided with papal bulls, letters of recommendation from king and bishop, and some of the cathedral's more precious relics. Then it was sent out on collection tours, which might extend from the nearby parishes to points as distant as Hungary, Sicily, Scotland, and Scandinavia. The dispatch of these envoys became a fund-raising ceremony in itself, with the clergy and

51

Processions such as the one in the fifteenth-century miniature at left were a familiar sight in medieval France, where sacred relics were carried through the city streets in order to raise money to erect cathedrals. The mania for building that swept the nation is illustrated in the 1448 illumination at right. Twelve churches — including the four in the intricate ornamental border — in honor of the twelve apostles are seen at various stages of completion.

populace forming processions and accompanying the missionaries to the gates of the city to speed them on their way.

One method of raising funds was quick, easy, and efficient, but unfortunately it was destined ultimately to undermine the moral integrity and unity of the Church. That method was the granting of indulgences in return for a pilgrimage to a church and an offering to its saints. An indulgence was supposedly only a pardon to a contrite sinner, which would relieve him of the temporal punishment for his sin; but it was widely understood to be a general remission of sins. Pope Urban II granted the first plenary indulgence to the soldiers of the First Crusade — and thus started a flood that the Church could not check. Soon "pardoners" were going about everywhere in Europe offering indulgences for trivial sums. The pardoners pocketed their commissions, the building funds of the cathedral chapters swelled, but the coinage of spiritual redemption inevitably became debased. By the time of the Reformation, the sale of indulgences had corrupted the sellers and become one of the central issues of the reformers. In a sense, the Church foundered on the rocks upon which the cathedrals grew.

Considering the competition, it is astonishing that these methods worked at all. For the whole of France was building cathedrals, and Italy, Germany, England, Bohemia, and even faraway Hungary were also entering the race. Yet for two hundred years the missionaries and the pardoners went from city to city, from fair to fair, throughout Europe, and those who had just given generously to build their own church somehow found it possible to give again for a distant cathedral

they could never hope to see — such was the love of Heaven, the fear of Hell and, it must be added, the relative prosperity of Western Europe in the twelfth and thirteenth centuries.

Everywhere, moreover, the novel Gothic style, begun by Suger at Saint-Denis and continued by Maurice at Notre-Dame de Paris, triumphantly displaced the Romanesque. At Senlis, Laon, Lisieux, Chartres, Meaux, Angers, Noyon, Poitiers, Soissons, and many smaller places a perpetual cloud of stone and mortar dust overhung the towns as the builders learned from, imitated, and strove to outdo one another.

At Paris the work proceeded steadily, at a reasonable pace. Maurice de Sully was a solid, deliberate man, not one to outrun his resources by a feverish initial campaign that would then lapse for years while new funds were frantically collected. Once the cornerstone was laid — perhaps by Pope Alexander in person — and the elaborate dedication ceremonies completed, Maurice matched outgo to income and employed just enough workmen to keep the cathedral growing briskly but not wastefully. The foundations were dug thirty feet deep and filled with the hard stone of Montrouge to take the enormous weight that would be raised upon them.

The chancel — choir and apse — was built first. For here the priests officiated, here the high altar must stand. Once the chancel was built, the church could function. As Maurice conceived them, choir and apse would be big enough and grand enough for the celebration of royal weddings, funerals, and victories even before the completion of the nave. By itself, in fact, the chancel formed a sizable church, 170 feet long and 157 feet wide, with the vaulting of the choir rising to

the unprecedented height of more than 100 feet. Four
tiers of windows — sapphire, ruby, topaz, and emerald
— poured jeweled light into the sanctuary. Auxiliary
altars were ranged against the curving outer wall of the
apse, and the ambulatory, the wide passageway that
swept around the eastern perimeter of the building,
was to be double-aisled.

Such a plan had already been attempted at Saint-
Denis. But the immense scale of the new Notre-Dame
multiplied the technical difficulties. The vaults were
higher and the spans wider than had so far been conquered by the new building style. Yet Maurice de
Sully and his architect were aiming for impressive
vistas, not to be spoiled by a multiplicity of supporting
members.

The problem was ingeniously solved by the spacing
of the pillars, and by combining simple transverse
arches with a system of triangular ribbing. The re-
sultant design was a triumph of both aesthetics and
practicality. It would be imitated again and again in
subsequent churches; but the clarity, grace, and noble
perspectives of the apse at Notre-Dame de Paris have
remained overwhelming. Yet this portion of the church
was built in less than twenty years. More important, it
set the dominant motif for the remainder of the cathedral, even though building continued well into the
fourteenth century.

When we stand in the apse today, we should be aware
of a number of later changes. To be sure, the basic
structure has not been tampered with, and all of the
columns are still those innocent round ones that art
historians have labeled Transitional. The builders left
behind the massive piers of the Romanesque but had

not yet learned to disguise the girth of their supports by the flutings, the crimpings, the host of tricks with form that we immediately identify as Gothic. These columns reveal at once how they were made. Twelve or thirteen uniform solid drums of hard stone are laid one above the other. Each column rests sturdily on a square base. Each is topped by a capital that is evidently meant to echo the Corinthian mode. But the classical acanthus leaves are simplified, almost rusticated. The same sort of columns were to be continued throughout the nave, but there they would be supplemented by a more typically Gothic pier, made up of a cluster of colonnettes.

It almost seemed that beginning the construction of Notre-Dame had regained the favor of Heaven for the Capetian dynasty. Two years after the laying of the cornerstone, all the bells in Paris burst forth in peals of joy, and the citizens rushed into the streets with torches and candles, creating such a sudden blaze of light that the whole city seemed afire. Alix of Champagne had borne Louis VII the male heir he had prayed for through three marriages and twenty-eight years as ruler of France. Gerald of Wales, who was then a student in Paris, vividly described the excitement that ran through the city at the birth of Philip Augustus:

The author of this work, being in the city, and then a young man in the twentieth year of his age, immediately leaped to the window from the couch on which he had stretched himself and fallen into his first sleep; and looking out, he saw two very poor old women in the street bearing torches . . . and exulting with joy. . . . And when he had inquired of them the cause of such commotion and exultation, one of them imme-

diately looked up at him and replied: "We have now a king given us by God, by whom disgrace and loss, punishment and grievous shame, confusion and sorrow in abundance, shall come upon your king."

Throughout the boyhood of Philip Augustus, Louis was engaged in an almost continuous struggle with his most powerful vassal, King Henry of England. Despite the disparity in wealth and power between the tiny Capetian monarchy and the vast Plantagenet empire, Louis managed to hold his own. Whenever he was driven to retreat by military force, he would remind Henry of his oath of vassalage — for Louis was technically Henry's overlord for his Continental lands. And Henry, a scrupulous observer of the feudal code by conviction and necessity — for he did not want to be a bad example to his own restive vassals and sons — invariably granted the requested truce.

Louis, to give him due credit, also tried to be scrupulous, but he lacked his rival's will and resources. In 1174, taking advantage of Henry's preoccupation with the revolt of his eldest son — which Louis himself had fomented — the French king invaded Normandy. He raised one of the largest armies that had been seen in Europe for many years and laid siege to the formidable city of Rouen. So large was their army that the French were able to split into three groups and thus divide the watch into three eight-hour periods. Finally a continuous, full-scale assault was launched. But instead of fighting without respite, the citizens of the populous city similarly apportioned their numbers and manned the walls in three shifts.

After many days of unremitting battle, the feast-day of Saint Lawrence arrived. Louis, who had a special

veneration for the martyr, ordered a day's truce, which
his heralds ceremonially announced. The citizens of
Rouen accepted gladly; there were gay celebrations of
the holiday, and a tournament was held outside the
city in full view of the French troops. The sight was too
much for the besiegers. Louis's allies and counselors
came to him and urged him to take advantage of this
priceless opportunity to steal up to the walls with scal-
ing ladders and take the city by surprise assault.

"Far be it from me to sully my royal honor with so
foul a stain," Louis at first replied. But he was soon
overborne by the arguments of his nobles. At last he
consented. Word was spread throughout the army by
whispers, and the advance began.

Fortunately for the citizens, some clerks in a tower
who were passing the time — perhaps with forbidden
dice — happened to look out the window and noticed
the preparations. They immediately began to ring
Ruvell, the great bell of Rouen, summoning the defenders to the walls. Hearing the clangorous warning,
the besieging army rushed forward, mounted ladders
already in place, and were shouting in triumph at the
summit of the wall — when they were counterattacked
by the soldiers who had been playing at battle outside
the walls. A violent struggle ensued; the defenders of
Rouen won, and the besieging army that had violated
the truce withdrew with heavy losses. Shortly afterward, King Henry came to the relief of the city.
Ashamed that he had been lured into breaking his
word, Louis no longer had the heart to continue the
fight. He and his vast army retreated with, as the
chronicler put it, "no other reward but dishonor for
such great labor."

Louis VII did not quite live to see the choir and
apse of Notre-Dame completed. An old man before he
reached sixty, he arranged for the coronation of his heir
at Reims but was himself unable to attend the ceremony. After a lingering illness, he died in the beloved
shadow of the new cathedral, in the very Cloister of
Notre-Dame where he had been raised as a child. His
contemporary William of Newburgh praised him as
"a man of fervent devotion toward God and singular
mildness toward his subjects, and also one who highly
reverenced men in holy orders." But, William added,
"he was rather more simple than became a monarch,
and in some of his actions he most clearly expressed the
truth of the Apostle's words, 'Evil communications corrupt good manners.' Indeed, by putting undue trust
in the counsels of certain nobles who cared too little
for what is honorable and just, he frequently sullied
his otherwise admirable character."

To his son Philip Augustus, Louis left the conquest
and absorption of the Angevin possessions on the Continent. His own greatest monument was the ring of
noble churches and cathedrals in and around Paris.
Saint-Denis, Sens, Vézelay, Noyon, Senlis, Laon, Reims,
Châlons-sur-Marne, Mantes — almost as many magnificent churches were begun or reconstructed during his
reign as there were towns and abbeys in the royal
domain.

In these cathedrals a new kind of music was replac-
ing the Gregorian plain chant whose powerful, straight-
forward recitative had seemed the musical reflection of
the foursquare, massive Romanesque churches. The
new polyphonic style, more rhythmical and more complex, full of surprises like the nascent Gothic, had

its origin at Notre-Dame de Paris. Leoninus and Perotinus, two composers of genius, made Paris the center of the musical world. Leoninus in his *Magnus Liber* provided enough two-voiced music to cover the whole round of the ecclesiastical year. Perotinus, suiting his compositions to the acoustic demands of the new choir of Notre-Dame, rewrote many of Leoninus's organums by adding more voices and interweaving them into intricate melodies.

With pomp and circumstance, the high altar of Notre-Dame was consecrated in 1182. Assisted by Maurice de Sully, the papal legate, Henri de Château-Marçay, mixed holy water and chrism and inscribed the requisite seven crosses upon the altar. Then the altar was washed, wiped, and rubbed once more with oil of catechumens and chrism. The incense was blessed, and a grain of incense was placed in each of the corners of the altar and at its center. Then, once more, came the scraping and cleansing, sprinkling of the altar cloth and ornaments with holy water, and censing of the altar. Only then could the first mass be celebrated at the new altar.

It was a high honor for Maurice de Sully to have the papal legate present at this important ceremony. It was a higher honor still, three years later, for him to have Heraclius, the Patriarch of Jerusalem, officiate in his new choir. To men of this era of Crusades, the patriarch was the greatest ecclesiastic in the world next to the pope. Heraclius, however, had not come in triumph but as a supplicant. The plight of the Latin Kingdom of Jerusalem, established by the victorious Europeans of the First Crusade, had grown pitiable; the Saracen armies, united at long last under the able rule of Saladin, were rapidly conquering one Christian outpost after another. Heraclius pleaded with Philip Augustus to undertake a new Crusade before the Holy City itself fell to the Moslems. But the shrewd young King of France responded with evasions; he was more interested in stirring up the sons of Henry II of England to renewed revolt against their father. The patriarch then went on to England to offer Henry II the keys to Jerusalem and the crown of the Latin Kingdom of Jerusalem itself if he would bring an army to save the jewel of Christendom. Henry provided money and some soldiers, but he too had no intention of leaving his own lands unguarded while the predatory King of France and his own still more predatory sons remained at home.

Two years later, in 1187, the inevitable but incredible tidings came: the "enemies of God" had taken Jerusalem. What was more, they had captured the True Cross and had almost wiped out the Latin Kingdom. Only the cities of Tyre, Antioch, and Tripoli remained in Christian hands. The entire Christian world mourned in despair for a time — and then began to burn with a new crusading fever. Even such wary and self-interested monarchs as Henry II and Philip Augustus were caught up in the universal passion. For the time being they buried their disputes and agreed to take the cross. But even while preparations for the new Crusade were going forward, Philip Augustus connived with Richard Coeur de Lion to launch a new attack upon the aging King Henry. Suddenly Richard and Philip became the best of friends; with their combined forces they overwhelmed the unprepared English king, harried him until he fell ill from exhaustion and humiliation, and

forced him to a surrender that broke his spirit. On July 6, 1189, Henry II, one of the greatest of English monarchs, died muttering to himself: "Shame, shame, shame on a conquered king." The leadership of the new Crusade was left in the hands of Philip Augustus of France and Richard Coeur de Lion, the new King of England.

The friendship between Philip Augustus and Richard died promptly with Henry II, for Richard inherited the Plantagenet interests and his father's conflicts with the Franks. The quarrels between the two young sovereigns, begun on the Continent and continued in Sicily, came to a head in the swollen and terrible encampment at Acre in the Holy Land. There, laying siege to the Saracens in the formidable walled city of Acre, besieged in their turn by Saladin's encircling army, a vast host of Crusaders suffered and died of famine, pestilence, and the unbearable heat. The arrival of Philip Augustus and Richard with fresh arms, food, and soldiers turned the tide. Acre was taken by storm, despite the Greek fire and burning pitch that poured down from the ramparts. But although Austrians, Franks, Germans, Normans, Provençals, Englishmen, and even Scandinavians from the recently converted realms of the far north participated in the assault, the credit for the capture of Acre went to Richard Coeur de Lion. He dominated the army of the Third Crusade with his flamboyant personality and conspicuous wealth — he had taxed England till it bled to equip his army, and on the way to the Holy Land he had replenished his treasury by taking Cyprus and selling it to the Templars. Both King Richard and King Philip Augustus fell ill with the quartan fever

that was ravaging the Crusaders. Richard stayed on, but Philip, wracked by disease, gnawed by envy and suspicion, decided to return home less than a month after the fall of Acre. Before Philip left, Richard made him swear a solemn oath that he would observe the Truce of God and protect the lands of the King of England as if they were his own.

The crusading fervor began to melt away after the taking of Acre and the departure of Philip Augustus. Although Richard stayed on for more than a year, reconquering the coast of Palestine and acquiring such a reputation that his very name struck terror in the hearts of the Saracens, he did not succeed in regaining Jerusalem. Eventually, in September 1192, he hastily made peace with Saladin — who died six months later — and in October set out for Europe. He had come within sight of Jerusalem, but he had failed in the Crusade's chief objective: to recapture the Holy City. At least, however, under the terms of the new peace treaty, Christian pilgrims would be able to visit the Holy Places unhindered.

Richard had reason to hasten home, for the affairs of his kingdom were in disorder. His barons were restive, his brother John was intriguing against him, and Philip Augustus — violating his oath — was attacking Richard's lands in Normandy. Had it not been for the imperiousness and good sense of Richard's mother, Eleanor of Aquitaine, his whole realm would have fallen apart in this crisis.

Richard set sail over perilous autumnal seas, in a time of unusual gales, and had the ill luck to suffer shipwreck on the coast of Istria. Trying to make his way home overland, he fell into the hands of Duke

Judging from the spirited joust at left between the helmeted Richard Coeur de Lion and the fierce, blue-faced Saladin, the Third Crusade was an enterprise consistent with the rules of chivalric warfare. In truth, the grim scene below of Richard massacring his Saracen hostages in the Holy Land is much closer to reality. From his balcony at left, Richard complacently observes the gruesome spectacle. Headless corpses are piled up beneath a platform on which two blindfolded men are about to be beheaded. Others await their turn, while soldiers lead the next victims to the ladder.

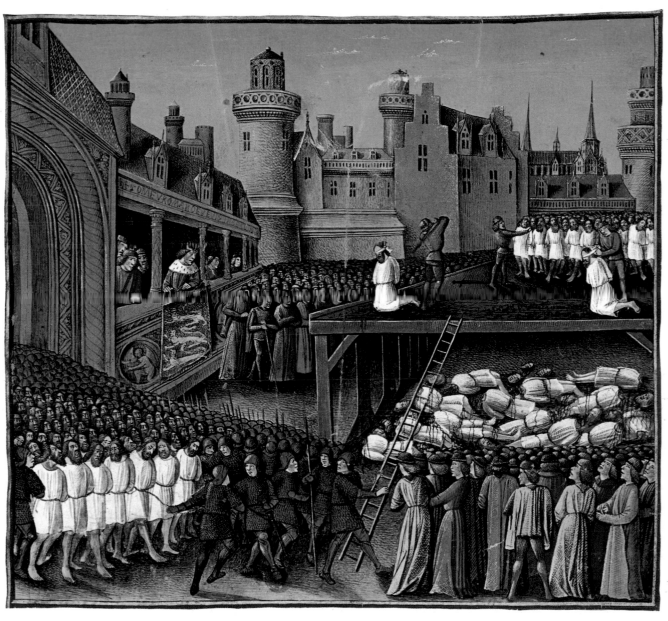

Leopold of Austria. Leopold turned him over, at a price, to his overlord, Emperor Henry of Hohenstaufen, who had succeeded Frederick Barbarossa. For two years thereafter Richard remained the most famous captive in the world, while his enormous ransom was being raised. Philip Augustus, defying both the pope and public opinion, exerted all his diplomacy to keep the King of England a prisoner as long as possible so he could pursue his war for recovery of the Angevin lands. All went well for the French until "the devil was loosed." Then Richard, free at last, rapidly threw Philip back on the defensive. By the closing year of the twelfth century Richard was beginning to threaten the île-de-France itself, when an arrow loosed in a petty quarrel with one of his vassals put a sudden end to the brilliant and sometimes unsavory career of Richard Coeur de Lion.

These stirring events — in the Holy Land and in Europe — inevitably slowed the work of building Notre-Dame de Paris, if only because the driving spirit behind it, Maurice de Sully, was so much preoccupied during the years of peril and warfare. Maurice served Philip Augustus much as Suger had served the king's father. Although Bishop Maurice does not appear ever to have become quite so important in the affairs of the realm as Suger had been, it is significant that Philip Augustus, before leaving for the Third Crusade, appointed Maurice one of the executors of his will. The Crusade and the subsequent war with England strained the resources of France. It became harder to raise funds for building after so much treasure had been poured into equipping the men who died in the disease-ridden squalor of the camp at Acre.

Nevertheless, Maurice had guarded his own revenues well. Early in his episcopate he completed his noble episcopal palace, which occupied the area between the new cathedral and the Seine. And throughout his long tenure as Bishop of Paris, work on the cathedral never ceased. By the time Maurice died in 1196, the great nave was substantially finished. As his last act of faith toward the cathedral he loved, Maurice provided in his will the sum of one hundred livres for the expenses of roofing. He left an equal amount to the "poor clerks" of the cathedral of Paris — for he himself had once, long ago, been just such a poor clerk, living on the charity of earlier bequests.

The nave of Notre-Dame de Paris benefited by the advances in the techniques of Gothic architecture that were being made all over France at this time. Outside, to support his 110-foot-high vaulting, the master of the work threw up a series of flying buttresses — perhaps for the first time, perhaps in imitation of what had been done at Saint-Denis and in smaller churches around the île-de-France (the question of priority is in dispute and perhaps can never be definitely settled). The sexpartite vaults — crossed ogives with a supplementary arch passing through their keystones — seemed to fling themselves toward Heaven, as if to reproduce in stone the soaring ambitions of Philip Augustus.

The double aisles of the choir continue through the nave, but there is a remarkable difference in the supporting columns. In the choir, these are uniform round shafts on square bases. In the long nave, the same scheme is followed in the central vessel. But the effect of a monotonous parade of pillars all exactly alike is broken by the inspired treatment of the central line

of columns separating the two aisles. Here simple shafts alternate with pillars surrounded by colonnettes that add both strength and grace. The changing rhythm of these columns is one of the greatest charms of the nave at Notre-Dame, for the colonnettes impose a vertical movement that contrasts beautifully with the horizontal feeling of the simple shafts, whose successive circular drums are plainly visible.

The capitals of the columns in the nave, as compared with those of the choir, illustrate the completed transition from Romanesque to Gothic. The floral patterns are still stylized, but there is a greater approach to realism, a greater fineness in the depiction of each leaf. Indeed, in spite of its vast size, fineness is the dominant characteristic of this nave. The structural members are thinner, leaner, less massive than those of the choir. The builders by then had acquired confidence in *opus francigenum,* or "French work," as Gothic architecture was generally called throughout Europe. They had a better understanding of the strength of colonnettes and pointed arches, and they had added to their already considerable arsenal of structural reassurances the vital device of the flying buttress.

With flying buttresses to support the upper parts of the nave, tribunes above the aisles were not strictly necessary. They were built nevertheless, for the sake of additional strength and consistency with the choir, and are among the most beautiful aspects of Notre-Dame de Paris. Wide, well-lighted, they are vaulted by simple crossed ogives that run down to engaged columns, between which the arcades are additionally supported by graceful, slender pilasters. Some of the capitals in these tribunes display long, narrow recurved leaves — first

examples of the crockets that were later to become so popular in Gothic architecture and that were used lavishly on the façade of Notre-Dame.

Under Maurice de Sully's successor, work on the façade began immediately after completion of the nave. As chance would have it, the new Bishop of Paris was named Eudes de Sully and came from the same town of Sully-sur-Loire as had Maurice. But there was no kinship between them, and in fact the two men were as different as pauper and prince. Eudes de Sully was a noble, related to many of the great secular and ecclesiastical lords of France and England. Indeed, Philip Augustus was his cousin; and Eudes de Sully as bishop had the rare courage to "obey God rather than man," as the biblical phrase so current at the time had it. What that meant in practice was that he opposed his king and obeyed the pope, who had placed the French realm under interdict to punish Philip for repudiating his second wife. In quarrels with the papacy, kings expected support from their own bishops. But Eudes de Sully immediately stopped services in the cathedral of Paris and enforced the interdict throughout his diocese.

But although his relations with Philip were often strained, as Maurice's had scarcely ever been, Eudes de Sully had one great advantage over his predecessor that redounded to the benefit of Notre-Dame: he was independently wealthy. He was also willing to devote his large means to the embellishment of his cathedral. The result was that the original design of the western façade was reconceived on a more ambitious scale — so much more ambitious that the façade ultimately took more years to build than had the choir and nave

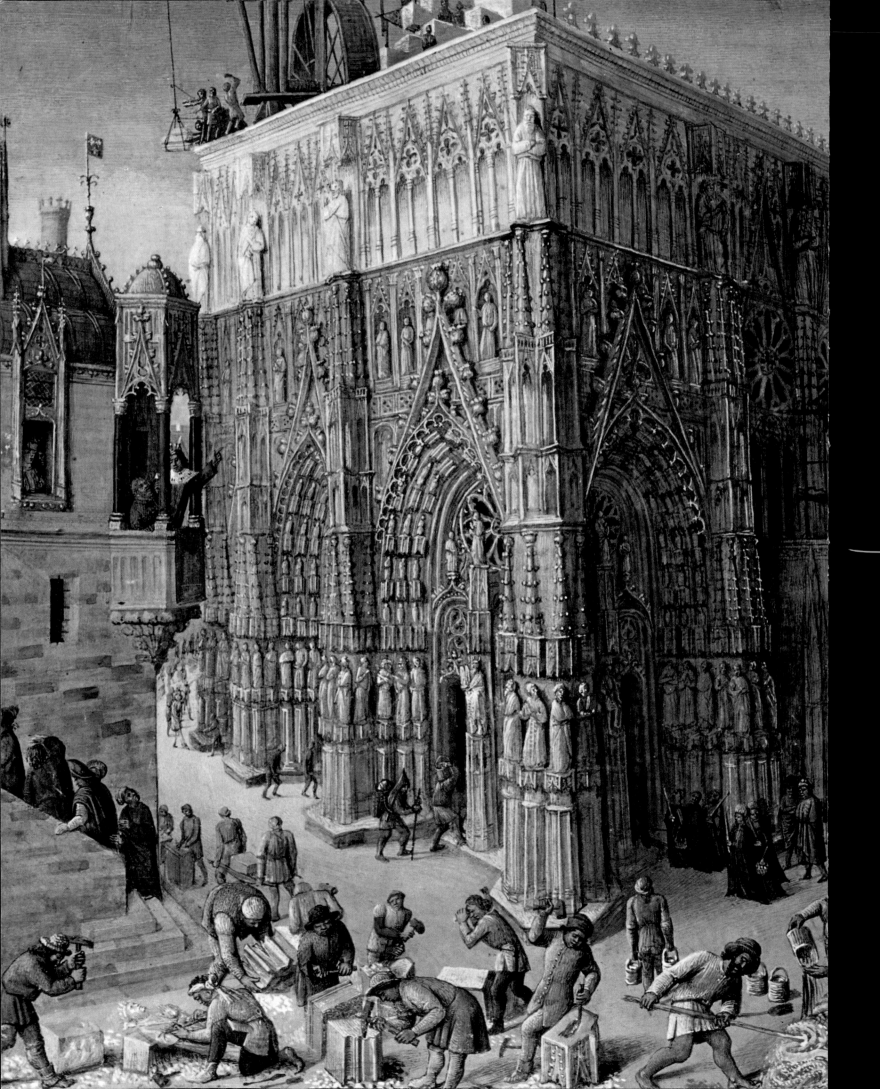

together.

It was during the first twenty-five years of the thirteenth century that the grandiose western façade was erected as far as the stage of the great rose. The magnificence of the façade harked back to Norman ancestors, particularly Saint-Etienne and La Trinité at Caen with their schemes of three portals and two towers. It is even possible that the ancient Christian basilicas of Syria influenced the design of the Paris façade — Crusaders and pilgrims would have seen these many times. Saint-Denis, Senlis, Noyon, Laon, and other churches of the Île-de-France likewise served as models. But for perfection of balance, harmony of parts, and beauty of detail, the western façade of Notre-Dame de Paris equals or surpasses all.

The three great portals, each set between a pair of buttresses, all differ somewhat in height and width as well as in sculptural subjects. The central portal, higher and wider than the other two, has suffered the most damage from time and man — those two great enemies of architectural monuments of which, Victor Hugo remarked, man is the worse. In 1771 the architect Jacques Soufflot destroyed the beauty of the portal by enlarging it so that processions with canopies could pass through. The nineteenth-century restoration permits us to see the portal in its original shape, but much of the sculpture is the work of Eugène Emmanuel Viollet-le-Duc and his pupils.

The subject, traditional for cathedrals, gives the central portal its name: the Portal of the Last Judgment. At the summit of the tympanum a majestic Christ sits in judgment upon the sinful and the good, whose souls are being weighed by Saint Michael in the upper lintel.

Two angels beside Christ hold the nails, lance, and cross (those sacred relics that the chivalry of France were trying to wrest from Saladin at the time the original sculptures were carved). A little lower than the angels, Mary and Saint John kneel before Christ to pray that mercy be shown to the human race. On the left side of the upper lintel, under Christ's upraised right hand, the saved rise to Heaven; on the right, the damned are being dragged down to Hell. The crowned souls of the just are being guided to Paradise by a lovely angel; a savage demon tugs at a long rope dragging the sinners downward. In the covings to the left of the tympanum Heaven and all its angels, patriarchs, saints, virgins, and doctors of the Church, are displayed; while on the right are chaos, horror, the ugly twisting and writhing shapes of Hell and all its demons.

Viollet-le-Duc's restorations on the pier, pillars, splays, and bases of the great central portal were as true to the originals as he could make them in the nineteenth century. A mere list of the subjects suggests the complexity of this religious art: Christ as teacher, the Liberal Arts, the Wise and Foolish Virgins, the Apostles, the Virtues and the Vices — a large segment of Christian doctrine and Christian history was incorporated into this one great portal.

Yet the central portal, with its wealth of sculpture, is only one of three. The Portal of Saint Anne, to the right, contains the oldest sculptures in the cathedral, as has already been noted. The lintels of this portal show scenes from the New Testament: the Annunciation, the Visitation, the Nativity, King Herod and the Magi, Saint Joachim and Saint Anne, and so on.

FACADE   OCCIDENTALE

This precise rendering of Notre-Dame's western façade was drawn by Eugène Emmanuel Viollet-le-Duc during the course of his nineteenth-century restoration of the cathedral. It clearly shows the major divisions of the exterior: the portals, from left to right, of the Virgin, the Last Judgment, and Saint Anne; the Gallery of Kings; the level of the rose window; and the upper gallery of open arcades. Between the towers is the slender flèche that rises over the crossing.

The statues below the lintel are reconstructions from the workshop of Viollet-le-Duc.

The left portal, the Portal of the Virgin, is distinguished from the others by the gable above the tympanum. As the whole church was consecrated to the Virgin, so also was one entire portal of the façade. Here was the place for those scenes recorded in the Apocrypha, which so stirred the imaginations of men in the twelfth and thirteenth centuries: the death, assumption, and coronation of the Mother of God. It is worth remarking that during those centuries, in which the Virgin was venerated with unprecedented fervor, two women wielded unprecedented political power in Europe: Eleanor of Aquitaine and her granddaughter, Blanche of Castile, the mother of Saint Louis of France.

The thirteenth-century tympanum of the Portal of the Virgin shows Mary's burial and assumption. Below this scene sit three kings of Judah, to emphasize Mary's royal ancestry, and three prophets, to recall the Old Testament prophecies of the coming to earth of Jesus Christ.

To the thirteenth-century mind, the Virgin provided the link between human lowliness and divine majesty. She had also incorporated into herself the goddesses of the ancient world, those seasonal goddesses like Ceres and Proserpine. Hence it was only natural that the pier should show in bas-relief the changing seasons and the ages of man, that the pillars should depict the months and their labors. A Bible in stone, a calendar in stone: the medieval cathedral tried, like the medieval summa, to be an epitome of all the knowledge that was needed for life and salvation.

Above the three portals, running across the entire façade, the builders of Notre-Dame created the Gallery of Kings. Here twenty-eight kings of Israel looked out over the Île de la Cité. The statues we now see are restorations, for in the French Revolution antiroyalist Paris saw the twenty-eight as kings of France, not Israel, and took them down. But if they misinterpreted the letter of the religious iconography, can it be said that they misinterpreted the spirit? The statues of the gallery may have depicted the kings of Israel, not France; but the sculptors had indeed been glorifying the only monarchy they knew. In the Gallery of Kings they were undoubtedly proclaiming their pride in the triumphs of the French monarchy, which had grown so notably in power and prestige during the first quarter of the thirteenth century.

On the western façade of Notre-Dame, symbolic statuary groupings of astonishing artistry tell the story of the New Testament in stone. At left is a close-up of the main portal, devoted to the Last Judgment. The majestic figure of Christ, presiding over the separation of the blessed from the damned, dominates the tympanum; another, more compassionate Christ, occupies the central pier. A detail from the upper lintel (below, near left) shows Saint Michael and Satan weighing souls, as an angel and a demon crouch beneath the scales of justice. The twisted bodies suffering the tortures of hell (below, at far left) are from the right-hand voussoirs of the portal. At right is the upper portion of the famed Portal of the Virgin. The tympanum depicts Mary's coronation; the upper lintel, her dormition in the presence of Christ, two angels, and the twelve apostles; and in the lower lintel are the seated figures of the three prophets and the three kings of Judea. Below is a detail of the stylized flourishes that form the grillwork of the Virgin's door. Spanning the entire width of the façade above the portals is the Gallery of Kings — a detail appears at right below. The twenty-eight statues of the kings of Israel, set in niched arches, are nineteenth-century works commissioned by Viollet-le-Duc to replace the originals, which were destroyed during the French Revolution.

While Maurice and Eudes de Sully had been devoting their talents and solicitude to Notre-Dame cathedral and the quarter around it, King Philip Augustus provided a setting for the majestic monument by improving the capital. The story goes that he was standing at his window one day when a cart, churning the muddy street below him, sent such foul odors to the king's nostrils that he forthwith ordered the streets of Paris to be paved. The work began at once, but like cathedral-building, it could not be completed in a day or a year. In fact, it continued steadily for 150 years. The quarrymen of the Île-de-France were kept fully employed on this and many other projects during the forty-three years of Philip's reign. The king erected a great wall, eight feet thick, strengthened by some five hundred towers, around the city. He built Les Halles to shelter the market traditionally held on the spot. The Louvre, too, was begun in Philip's reign.

Along with the fortification and embellishment of the capital, Philip Augustus pursued a vigorously expansionist foreign policy that abruptly altered the balance of power in Europe. With Richard Coeur de Lion out of the way and luckless John Lackland on the English throne, Philip rapidly conquered Normandy and most of the other Plantagenet possessions on the Continent. He completed this conquest, significantly, in the same year that Eleanor of Aquitaine — who had remained the *grande dame* of England past her eightieth year — died and was laid to rest beside her husband, Henry II, in Fontevrault Abbey.

That same year, 1204, there were Frenchmen in the streets of Constantinople, gathering "booty so great that none could tell you the end of it: gold and silver, and vessels and precious stones, and samite, and cloth of silk, and robes of vair and gray, and ermine, and every choicest thing found upon the earth. . . . Never since the world was created had so much booty been won in any city."

Those Frenchmen were part of the army of the Fourth Crusade, which like the third had set out to retake Jerusalem. It ended by capturing the Christian city of Constantinople and overrunning a sizable portion of the Byzantine Empire for the benefit of Venice. The Latin Empire, which the Crusaders established in Byzantium, ruled over a sullen populace. Threatened from without by the Moslems, it lasted for only half a century. But during that time French interests, bound together by intricate familial ties and feudal relationships, extended from the English Channel across Europe and through the Adriatic and the Aegean seas to the shores of the Black Sea.

Such conquests were temporary, however, and did not directly affect the growth of the royal domain and the increasing power of a centralized monarchy in France. Another misdirected crusade, no less motivated by lust for booty, had a more lasting effect upon the fortunes of the French people and the ultimate destiny of France. That was the Albigensian Crusade, one of the more somber chapters in the history of France. It was named after the city of Albi in southern France, which for a time was the center of the Catharist heresy.

The general intellectual awakening of the twelfth century, the renewal of contacts between Christendom and the outside world, and the growing secular influence of the papacy had stimulated severe criticism of the Church both from within and from without. Some

Against Heathen and Heretic

of the most fervent and orthodox churchmen of the age, like Saint Bernard, denounced the venality and luxurious tastes of many ecclesiastics with a fury that almost matched that of the heretics. Reforms were initiated, but the need for reform remained perennial. The new orders of monks, such as the Cluniacs and Cistercians, began in simplicity and austerity but eventually succumbed to the temptations of wealth and display. The higher prelates were also powerful secular lords with expensive tastes and interests that compromised their religious mission. The Crusades themselves involved the Church in so much political maneuvering, in so many concessions to expediency, that they undermined the spirituality of the papacy even as they strengthened its secular authority.

It is against this background that the rise of heresy in northern Italy and southern France must be viewed. Heretics by definition are those who find themselves on the losing side in disputes over dogma and church policy. Protestantism ceased to be a heresy and became a separate church because it won a few battles. The people of Languedoc were not so fortunate; history therefore speaks of them as "heretics." But in fact they came very close to setting up an independent church of their own before they went down to defeat in a bloody and merciless war.

The Catharist or Albigensian church originated from two principal strands: from reformist movements within Catholicism, such as that of the Waldensians, also called "the poor men of Lyons" (who preached doctrines not unlike those later taken up by the Franciscans); and from ancient Manichean beliefs which had lingered in the Balkans, northern Italy,

southern France, and Spain. The Manicheans held that this world was the creation of the power of evil, which they saw as engaged in a perpetual struggle with the power of good. Priests and the whole organization of the official church were, in their view, but instruments of evil. Absolute pacifism, near or total vegetarianism, abstinence, and continence were among their tenets. The Catharist preachers needed only to point to the corrupt lives of many members of the clergy for their arguments to be convincing to the laity. And those preachers themselves were so fanatically ascetic — to the point, so it was alleged, of sometimes voluntarily starving themselves to death in order to escape this evil world — that their example won them countless followers in a region noted for its luxury and easy living.

It was difficult to found a church upon such doctrines, but the Cathars (the word comes from Greek, meaning "the Pure") succeeded by certain compromises that made room for the salvation of ordinary humanity. The leaders or bishops freed themselves from evil by becoming *perfecti*, leading lives of utmost purity. They in turn could pass on salvation to the faithful by a laying on of hands called the *consolamentum*, or consolation, which would usually be administered to the layman just before death. This, in a way, was a reversion to the primitive Christian practice of deathbed baptism.

The new doctrine began winning many adherents around the middle of the twelfth century. By the beginning of the thirteenth century it had become so widespread in the countryside around Albi, and in much of southern France all the way to the Pyrenees and beyond, that Catholic churchmen became seri-

ously alarmed. When papal legates and missionaries failed to sway the heretics, Pope Innocent III called for a crusade against these fellow Christians. The immediate pretext was the assassination of a papal legate by one of the officers of the Count of Toulouse.

The war that began in 1208 was marked by unprecedented cruelty. The northern French barons under the leadership of Simon de Montfort deliberately embarked on a policy of sheer terrorism, as a contemporary noted:

> The nobles of France, clergy and laity, princes and marquises, agreed among themselves that whenever a château they invested refused to surrender and had to be taken by force, the inhabitants were to be put to the sword and slain; thinking that afterwards no man would dare to stand out against them by reason of the fear that would go abroad when it was seen what they had already done.

One consequence of this policy was the terrible slaughter at Béziers, in which the entire population of the city was killed. It was here that the Cistercian abbot Arnald-Amalric, queried on how to distinguish Catholics from heretics, is supposed to have said: "Slay them all; God will take care of his own." Whether or not these words were ever spoken, they express the spirit in which the war was conducted. And as a further consequence, heretics and Catholics united to defend their land against the invader.

The Albigensian Crusade developed into a protracted war of conquest on the one side, a stubborn territorial defense on the other. It continued for more than a generation, until the rich and prosperous civilization of Languedoc lay shattered, its cities burned, its

vines uprooted, its flourishing commerce ruined, its independence gone. Butchered by ruthless mercenaries, fanatical knights, and the agents of the newly created Inquisition, the heretics were exterminated. The smoke of burning faggots and flesh rose above the whole Midi. Only a few heretics escaped into the mountains of Savoy and Piedmont — where their persecution continued down to the nineteenth century.

It soon became clear that the real object of the war was annexation by the French crown of the powerful county of Toulouse. That aim was undeviatingly pursued by Philip Augustus until his death in 1223, by his son Louis VIII, and after his death three years later by Blanche of Castile, who governed France during the minority of her son Louis IX, the future Saint Louis. The counts of Toulouse, Raymond VI and Raymond VII, attempted to preserve their independence by asserting their Catholic orthodoxy while defending their Catharist subjects. They turned and twisted, sometimes hunting or pretending to hunt heretics, sometimes summoning their heretic vassals to join them in the defense of their country. Ultimately it proved impossible for the counts to walk the diplomatic and theological tightrope. Although Count Raymond VII held Toulouse against overwhelming odds, the devastation of the countryside and the frequent betrayals by his Catholic clergy ultimately forced him to capitulate. He agreed to a humiliating treaty, yielding his independence in return for peace and a lifting of the ban of excommunication that had been imposed upon him. On April 12, 1229, the defeated Count of Toulouse came to Notre-Dame de Paris to be reconciled to the Church.

The decorously draped stone figure at left, from
Eleanor of Aquitaine's tomb in Fontevrault Abbey,
belies the vigor and passion of the woman who had
been queen of both France and England. As an
impediment to monarchical authority, Eleanor's
native province was rivaled only by its neighbor
Toulouse. The thirteenth-century bas-relief below
depicts the crown's savage campaign to subdue that
rebellious region. Against overwhelming odds, the
inhabitants (on the right) desperately maneuver
a catapult in an effort to scale the palisade that
separates them from their besiegers.

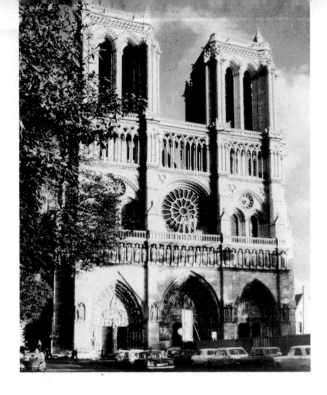

All around the parvis outside the bright new façade of Notre-Dame seats had been erected for the dignitaries. The ladies, nobles, and prelates were decked out in their most brilliant robes. Queen Mother Blanche and fourteen-year-old King Louis sat side-by-side on thrones, flanked by bishops and barons. In their presence, Raymond VII signed the act of surrender. Then he was stripped to his shirt and breeches, a cord was placed around his neck, and he was dragged down the whole length of the nave to the high altar. There, to complete his shame, he knelt and was scourged by the cardinal-legate of the pope. After that humiliation — surely one of the most dramatic of the many stirring scenes that were to take place in Notre-Dame de Paris over the centuries — the count was held prisoner in the Louvre for another six months.

Raymond survived to emerge from prison and lead other fruitless rebellions perhaps only because the queen mother and the royal party needed him as a possible counterpoise to other powerful barons. Blanche of Castile — a foreigner, exceedingly if not excessively devoted to the Church, more ready to listen to the advice of her Spanish retainers than her French counselors — had inherited the beauty, the presence, and the iron will of her grandmother Eleanor of Aquitaine. These qualities enabled her, in a time of unending feudal plots and counterplots, to maintain her position and save the kingship for her son. She taught him well, and she made him a judicious king, concerned for the welfare of his humblest subjects. Unfortunately, she also imbued him with such intense piety that he led the nation on two more disastrous Crusades.

By the time Louis IX became King of France, the rose window of the western façade of Notre-Dame had been completed. This magnificent wheel of stone, like a huge halo around the head of the Virgin whose statue poises on the balustrade in front of it, is one of the miracles of thirteenth-century architecture. The rose is thirty-two feet in diameter — the largest of its kind when it was erected — and the builders confronted the triple problem of sustaining the immense pressure of the surrounding stone upon so large a gap in the wall, of dividing the space into approximately equal areas, and of providing room enough for the glass, so that the window would serve its function of admitting a flood of colored light to the interior.

They solved these problems ingeniously by arranging slender colonnettes like the spokes of a wheel all around the central oculus. These spokes run to a second circle of trefoiled arches on which rests a second series of colonnettes. But here, in between each radius, an additional colonnette to the outer rim has been inserted. The elegant result is approximately equal division of the space and tremendous strength in the whole structure. Functionalism alone, however, was never the aim of the medieval builder; and the effect of this rose is one of singular harmony, restfulness, and confidence. The loveliness of the stone tracery is enhanced by the sturdy semicircular arches, ornamented with innumerable crockets that surround the upper half of the window. These arches again rest on columns that recapitulate the theme of the window itself. So also do the slender columns of the bays between the buttresses to either side of the rose. The wheel theme also is recapitulated in the two blind roses in the tympanum of each bay; the crockets of the semicircular arch are

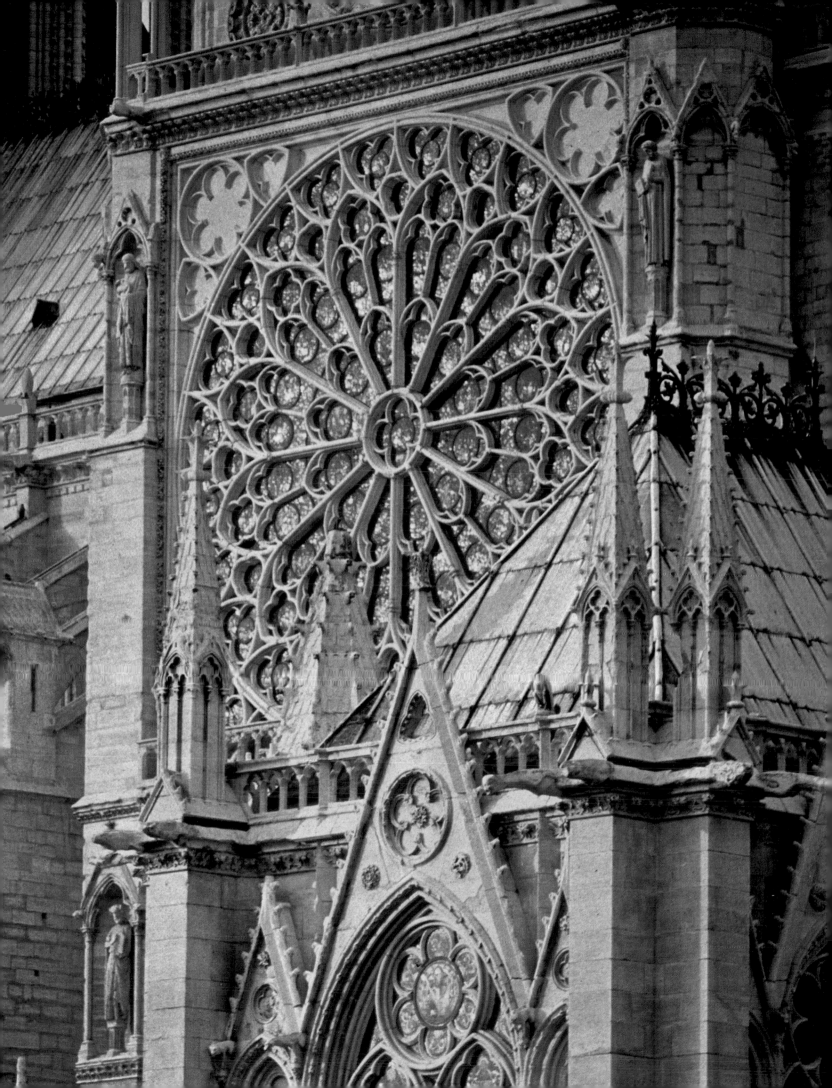

repeated in the cornice that extends across the entire façade above the rose.

Seen from the interior, the western rose is somewhat disappointing. A good third of it is obscured by organ pipes that were installed there in the eighteenth century. And all the original glass has vanished; what we now see are nineteenth-century restorations. Although they are good work, they remain only a dim simulacrum of the thirteenth-century glass. One realizes that fully if one stands at the crossing of the transept and looks up at the rose of the northern façade. Here, in the glorious rose window built by Jean de Chelles around 1250, the gemlike glass — blue, red, green, brown, and yellow, but predominantly blue — is almost all of the thirteenth century.

Without binoculars, the subjects depicted on the northern rose are difficult to make out from the ground, but the colors, and the light that falls through them onto the church floor, are breathtaking. Mary is in the center of the wheel, of course; in the circles around her are the kings and prophets of the Old Testament. The window is larger than the western rose and contains proportionately more stone to glass; but it looks no heavier. The whole enormous structure rests upon the frail clerestory windows below it, but the lacelike tracery and the small trefoiled roses in the corners distribute the weight so perfectly that no sagging or cracking has appeared in seven centuries.

The southern rose, unfortunately, did not fare so well, perhaps because exposure to the sun weakened it more than the others, perhaps because normal maintenance was neglected on this side. At any rate, this rose began to buckle in the sixteenth century. An eighteenth-century reconstruction made matters worse, and the whole façade crumbled. In the nineteenth century Viollet-le-Duc decided that the trouble lay in the inadequate buttressing. He therefore reinforced the buttresses and rebuilt the entire wall, creating a new southern rose in the original style. Here is our chance to judge his merits as a restorer. The glass, predominantly red in keeping with tradition, is deceptively good. The expert may recognize it as nineteenth-century, but the overwhelmed lay observer is not likely to question its authenticity.

The stone tracery follows the same pattern as that of the other roses. It casts an interesting light on the reverse "progress" in architecture. For Viollet-le-Duc, with all the resources of nineteenth-century engineering science behind him, found it necessary to make his stone framework thicker and therefore somewhat clumsier than that of the medieval roses. Yet it is scarcely surprising that he could not compete with the thirteenth-century builders. For by the reign of Louis IX the new Gothic style had become the native language of France's architects. They were completely at home in it, had been working in the style for generations, son learning from father, apprentice from master, and had developed a boldness and assurance that enabled them to use stone almost as we use steel today. The passion for more and more light, ever leaner supports, had seized them all. Notre-Dame was brand-new, as cathedrals went, but to these thirteenth-century master builders it already looked antiquated, outmoded. And so, even before the structure was complete, they began modernizing it.

Around 1230 the original buttresses were replaced

by the immense scapular arches that give Notre-Dame its characteristic appearance. Along with this operation, lateral chapels were installed along both sides of the nave to take advantage of the space between the upright buttresses. More light was sought by increasing the amount of glass in the clerestory. During the thirteenth century much of the wall between the buttresses was removed and the opening was almost entirely filled with glass: a procession of twin lancet windows each surmounted by a miniature rose. Shortly afterward, the thirteenth-century north and south roses, which had been about eighteen feet in diameter, were also removed. Because of the installation of the lateral chapels, the transept façades were no longer in line with the rest of the structure. New façades were now built and the present vast roses — perhaps twice the diameter of the old ones — were installed in the north and south façades. But the traditional color scheme was kept: the north rose predominantly blue, the south an exquisite pink developed especially in the Paris glass workshops.

Colored glass had become a decisive element of the new architecture. The row upon row of immense, multicolored windows glowing within the dusk of lofty vaults made these thirteenth-century cathedrals like no buildings known before or since. The Middle Ages loved glittering things, shiny materials, strong colors, as we may see by the vast stores of jeweled, enameled, gilded objects kept today in museums or church treasuries. Yet colored glass outdid all other works of art in brilliance. The great Norman-Sicilian churches sheathed their walls in mosaic. The Romanesque churches had been brightened with wall paintings. In

75

Italy, the possibilities of colored marble — white, green, pink, and black — gave churches a suave richness. But neither mosaic nor paintings nor marble could begin to equal the jeweled intensity of French stained glass. As sunlight struck the outside of the church from any direction or at any angle, the interior was emblazoned with shimmering veils of colored light. Even on dark days the windows fulfilled their expository function, telling stories from the Old and New Testaments, celebrating saints and heroes, and commemorating the benefactors of the church — those members of the royal house or of the local nobility and the prosperous guildsmen who contributed generously to the window fund.

With each of the many windows further subdivided into panels, medallions, circlets, and niches, the stained glass formed a vast picture book which could repay a lifetime of study. But seen all together, the glass was overwhelming. Thanks to it, the inside of the church became miraculous, supernatural, the nearest approximation man could make on earth of the divine city promised to the faithful after death. When stained-glass windows filled entire bays of the clerestory, the cathedrals of the thirteenth century proclaimed the underlying principles of creation and were a visible sign of the power and perfection of the Creator.

But even as we admire these miracles, we must remember that the windows were made by men. The skills involved had reached a high degree of development. Color was infused into the molten glass itself — cobalt yielding the vast range of blues; iron oxide with added gold, the ruby reds; silver oxides, the yellows. But the same additives would also, in lesser or greater proportions, at higher or lower temperatures, produce purples or greens. The glassmakers commanded an astonishing number of these chemical tricks, secrets never written down and lost in subsequent centuries. Only in the middle of the nineteenth century, under the inspiration of Viollet-le-Duc, did the new scientific chemists laboriously analyze the composition of the glass and reconstruct the manner of its making. It then became evident that the very accidental nature of the process, the impurities of the ingredients, the lack of uniformity in each sheet of glass — which might be wavy, thick or thin, full of blisters and bubbles — had a great deal to do with the liveliness of the final effect. Glass made according to tested formulae and under controlled temperatures turned out to be a sorry imitation of the real thing. And then the lead armatures in which the panes of glass were set like so many jewels were also subject to infinite variations of coarseness and fineness, curvature or flatness. The soldering of the joints could be done neatly or roughly, and this too influenced the effect.

Before the final assembly, the colored glass was trimmed to size either by heating or cutting with a diamond, and it was then painted with the requisite details. Folds were painted into the garments, features upon faces, leaves upon trees. This was essentially an enameling process, utilizing a mixture of cullet (scrap glass), copper, and so-called Greek sapphire, dissolved in a vehicle of wine or urine. The second baking of the glass again produced surprises and idiosyncrasies, which became the despair of later scientific ages when they attempted to match the effects.

A small corps of artists was responsible for the designs. The stamp of certain masters can be seen in the

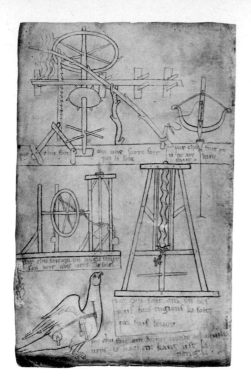

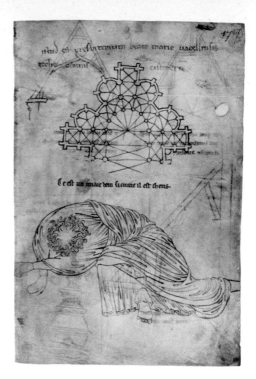

windows of a host of churches in the Île-de-France and beyond. Perhaps only a few workshops turned out all the stained glass. These shops had to be situated close to the raw materials — river sand was needed for the glass itself and forests to provide ample charcoal for the smelting. Chartres had the most notable workshop of all. Its glass was greatly in demand and exported as far as Canterbury in England. But there is reason to believe that the Chartres workshop employed Parisian artisans. For Paris, as the royal city, was the most active center of the decorative arts and attracted the finest craftsmen. Illuminators of manuscripts provided the king and court with psalters and books of hours; weavers of tapestries made vestments and altar cloths; goldsmiths and jewelers fashioned the reliquaries that were growing ever more elaborate.

It remained for the saintly King Louis — who washed the feet of beggars, submitted to frequent flagellation, attended mass twice daily, and thought he was doing his friends a favor by presenting them with hair shirts — to create the most elaborate reliquary of all. Louis heard that the Latin emperor in Constantinople was willing to sell the Crown of Thorns, the most precious relic in his possession. Mostly out of piety, but partly with the political aim of strengthening the Latin Empire, Louis agreed to the purchase — and raised part of the sum by a special tax on the Jews of Paris. But while the emperor was in France accepting King Louis's offer, his uncle in Constantinople had pawned the relic to a Venetian businessman. The Crown of Thorns, nevertheless, was redeemed for the vast sum of 177,300 livres and brought to Paris enclosed in three caskets like an Egyptian mummy, one of wood, one of silver,

and one of gold. With the whole population of Paris watching, the king and his brother, barefoot and in tunics, carried the precious burden into the cathedral of Notre-Dame.

The king wanted the relic near him, however, and soon he had it moved from Notre-Dame to the chapel of Saint Nicholas, within the palace. But when still more relics began arriving from Constantinople — a piece of the True Cross, the blade of the Holy Lance, the Holy Sponge — it became obvious that the old chapel was not splendid enough to house so many sacred objects. It was torn down, and within seven years — from 1241 to 1248 — the Sainte-Chapelle was built, its walls virtually all of blue and red glass. In the upper chapel Louis himself would frequently show the relics to the assembled notables.

Louis IX lavished donations upon the poor, upon the Hôtel Dieu, the chief hospital of Paris, and of course upon Notre-Dame de Paris. He managed to keep peace among his barons and with the sovereigns of Europe by sheer force of moral authority. But although his reign was peaceful at home, on the whole, his piety led him to embark upon terribly costly adventures *outre-mer*. In 1244, when he was in his thirtieth year, Louis fell so gravely ill that the ladies in attendance upon him disputed whether to draw the sheet over his face, for some thought him already dead. But he recovered, and as soon as he regained the power of speech he vowed that he would go on a Crusade. Horrified, his mother, Blanche, begged him not to go, and she even persuaded the pope to release the king from his vow. But Louis had rigid notions of honor. After lengthy preparations — which included transforming Aigues-

Mortes into a port from which the expedition could
sail — Louis embarked in 1248.

The aim of the Seventh Crusade was the conquest of
Egypt, regarded as the key to the Holy Land. All began
auspiciously with the capture of Damietta, but plague
and heat took their toll of the Crusaders as usual. The
campaign ended with the capture of Louis himself.
Threatened with torture by the Saracens, Louis calmly
replied that he was their prisoner and they could do as
they wished with him. The Sultan of Egypt, impressed
by his demeanor, agreed to ransom him for a million
gold bezants (500,000 livres). Louis consented to pay
the sum for his men; since it was beneath a king's
dignity to barter himself for coin, he would surrender
Damietta in return for his own release. "When the
sultan heard this he said. 'By my faith, this Frank is
large-hearted not to have bargained over so great a
sum! Now go and tell him that I will deduct a hundred
thousand livres from the ransom.' "

Louis was large-hearted in almost all his dealings.
While lingering in the Holy Land for four years after
his release from captivity, he fortified the cities of
Caesarea, Jaffa, and Sayette at his own expense. After
his return to France, he voluntarily restored to Henry
III of England some of the lands that Philip Augustus
had won. He endowed abbeys, almshouses, and hospitals everywhere in France, built lodgings for the
blind near Paris, and created the first home for women
who were euphemistically called *Filles-Dieu,* in which
he placed "a great multitude of women who, through
poverty, had lapsed into the sin of incontinence."

In spite of his piety, Louis was by no means priest-
ridden. He restrained the greed and ambition of his
bishops and archbishops, often rebuffing them as his
grandfather Philip Augustus had done. At one time
the ecclesiastics complained that sentences of excommunication were no longer effective. They asked
the king to employ his secular power to sustain these
sentences. Louis promptly replied that he would gladly
do so — if they gave him the right to judge whether
the sentences were just. The churchmen answered that
they could not allow this, since they alone were supposed to judge in spiritual matters. In that case, the
king retorted, he could not help them. For if their
sentences were unjust, as they sometimes proved to be
(and he gave examples), he would be acting "contrary
to God and against right."

The fact was that, in spite of his mild disposition,
Louis succeeded in pushing forward the policy initiated
by his great-grandfather Louis VII and so notably continued by Philip Augustus. That is, he extended the
sway of the French monarchy to the point that it became more powerful than any single noble or coalition
of vassals. Under Louis, France acquired a true central
government and at least the beginnings of a real
civil service. The king's court, the *curia regis,* began
dividing into government departments; the king's
household was developing into a bureaucracy. The importance of Paris increased as the government reached
out to all corners of the land through the king's
enquêteurs, emissaries from the court who traveled
about the country acting on the complaints of citizens
and inquiring into the conduct of local administrators.
In effect, Louis was reinstating in France the system
of *missi dominici* that had held Charlemagne's empire
together more than four centuries earlier.

In a lintel from the north façade (near right), the Virgin flees Egypt on a donkey. Her coronation scene appears in the tympanum of the Red Portal (far right). And within the cathedral (center), a graceful and ethereal Mary holds the Infant in her arms.

One of the most signal developments of the age of Saint Louis was an inadvertent by-product of his character and his rule. This was the rise of that complex code of behavior known as chivalry. The ideal of the courteous knight, protector of widows and orphans, defender of God and his liege lord, a man skilled in song and verse, adept at games and storytelling, consumed with passion for a lady he could never hope to possess — this ideal knight never existed outside the romances. Nevertheless, such notions made their way from Languedoc to northern France along with returning soldiers and impoverished troubadours. Saint Louis himself, though guilty of discourtesies toward his wife, was widely regarded as the paragon of the knightly ideal. Despite his concern for the poor, he maintained a proper princely state at table and in the appurtenances of his court. He was gentle with his subjects, honorable in his dealings with friend and foe alike, and would not break his plighted word even when it had been given to an "enemy of God." His example, and the long period of domestic peace during his reign, fostered the social arts that were bound up with the notion of chivalry.

Whether the actual status of women improved under the influence of chivalry is a much-debated question. As in earlier, ruder times, heiresses continued to be virtually bought and sold for economic reasons. But women often governed feudal estates while the men were away on the Crusades; and such strong women as Blanche of Castile and Louis's queen, Marguerite of Provence, must have provided an example to the less fortunate members of their sex. And there seems little doubt that the fervent devotion to the Virgin Mary

reflected at least some changes in the social structure. For at the same time Mary began to be adored like a human as well as a divine queen.

The new humanization of the Virgin is expressed in the charming statue of her that stands on the pier of the portal in the northern façade. Here the treatment is far more realistic than the august, hieratic Mary of the western façade. The Queen of Heaven stands leaning slightly to the right, looking at her son (the statue of the infant Jesus has not survived) with a singularly human tenderness. In the lintel of the same portal there is another Virgin Mary, equally humanized. The subject is the Nativity; ox and ass warm the Babe with their breath. Mary lies raised on one elbow, head cupped in her hand, wearing the dreamy expression of any mother meditating on her son's future.

There are still more Marys on the portal of the north façade. In the second tier of the tympanum the Heavenly Queen appears at last, the Mary of miracles, interceding for the deacon Theophilus, who has sold his soul to the devil in return for worldly goods and honors. Stricken by remorse and terror, Theophilus prays fervently to the Virgin, whereupon she snatches from Satan the pact signed in blood.

Yet another Virgin may be seen over the small door that enters the third bay of the choir, a short distance farther down the rue du Cloître Notre-Dame. Known as the Red Portal, from its painted doors, it provided a convenient entrance from the cloister for members of the chapter. In the tympanum an angel is placing a crown upon Mary's head, while Jesus blesses his mother; this is a repetition of the scene on the western façade. But our interest focuses upon the two kneeling

figures who represent the donors of the Red Portal: Louis IX and Queen Marguerite.

These statues may have been carved long before they were placed above the door some time between 1265 and 1267. For they show a youthful and handsome royal pair, when in fact Louis was by this time past fifty and nearing the end of his life. In 1270, so weak he could neither walk nor ride, he embarked on a new Crusade, the Eighth Crusade. As on the Seventh Crusade, he let himself be diverted from the true object: the Holy City. His brother, Charles of Anjou, persuaded him to attack Tunis. Summer heat and plague destroyed his army, and Louis himself died on August 25, 1270. His bones, returned to France, were carried to Notre-Dame in solemn procession and then buried at Saint-Denis.

Some of Louis's most loyal vassals did not accompany him on that last Crusade. A new spirit was in the air, an antagonism toward the Church, which had urged men on to wasteful foreign adventures or subverted the very meaning of crusading by "commuting" the crusaders' vows to allow them to attack fellow-Christians. Popular disgust with the futility of the cause to which Louis had sacrificed his riches and his health was vividly expressed by one of the foremost writers of the age, the trouvère Rutebeuf. A gifted forerunner of François Villon, Rutebeuf was essentially a poet of the people. He did not mince words in his attacks on the friars or in his condemnation of crusading:

Am I to leave my wife and children, all my goods and inheritance, to go and conquer a foreign land which will give me nothing in return? I can worship God

just as well in Paris as in Jerusalem. . . . All you people, great and small, who go on pilgrimage to the Promised Land, ought to become very holy there; so how does it happen that the ones who come back are mostly bandits?

Twenty-one years after the death of King Louis IX, the last Christian possession in Palestine was lost. The great age of the Crusades was over, and the age of the Church's hegemony was fast fading. At the beginning of the thirteenth century Pope Innocent III had wielded a virtual dictatorship over the secular rulers of Europe. During the sixty years after Innocent's death the Church seemed to be consolidating its gains on all fronts. The Inquisition had wiped out heresy; the new Dominican and Franciscan orders exercised close control over dangerous thinking in theology. Thomas Aquinas and the other great scholastics, many of them associated with the University of Paris, diverted the potentially dangerous philosophy of Aristotle and the new trend toward scientific thinking into channels of orthodoxy. The Church had demonstrated its capacity to collect vast sums for buildings, for Crusades, for an enormous administrative apparatus, and for wars conducted by the papacy itself. All over Europe its possessions, tithes, and exactions had increased enormously.

But in the very process of acquiring such power the Church set in motion countervailing forces, both within itself and among the peoples it dominated. A growing middle class with a rising sense of national consciousness resented what it regarded as taxation for the benefit of a foreign power, with the ensuing drain of capital toward Rome. The feudal nobility had largely infiltrated the higher ranks of the clergy and had brought with it into the Church its family concerns and secular habits. The kings, who on the whole had successfully established central governments that overrode provincial interests — this was especially true for France and England — would no longer brook interference in domestic affairs from churchmen at home or popes in Rome.

The brewing conflict came to a head at the beginning of the fourteenth century, during the reigns of Philip the Fair in France and Edward I in England. Both monarchs needed money for their wars against each other; both resorted to taxation of the Church and confiscation of the funds and property of monastic orders. When Pope Boniface VIII protested and restated the ancient papal claims to supremacy over secular rulers, Philip the Fair ordered him arrested. The physical attack on the pope in his palace at Anagni in central Italy horrified Europe — and also marked a break in the long tradition of cordial relations between France and the papacy. The aging pontiff was soon released, but the shock brought him to his grave.

In the confused maneuverings that followed Boniface's death and the brief reign of an interim pope, Philip the Fair succeeded in dominating the College of Cardinals. A French archbishop was elected and took office as Clement V in 1305, but he did not dare to proceed to Rome. He established his curia at Avignon — and thus began what was later called the Babylonian Captivity of the Church.

Avignon was technically situated in the Holy Roman Empire, but French language, culture, and influence prevailed there, and for the next seventy years the papacy was largely subservient to the rulers of France. In Avignon, to be sure, the popes were safe from the unpredictable mobs and the warring noble families of Rome. But Avignon lacked the aura of imperial authority that Rome had retained in spite of all the city's vicissitudes through the centuries. Without Rome, the Roman Church could not securely hold the loyalty and love of Europe's believers. Ultimately, the fabric of the entire Church was weakened.

For the time being, however, religious life turned inward, toward the national churches. In Paris, efforts were made to finish the remodeling of the cathedral, in spite of Philip the Fair's foreign wars, debasement of the currency, and heavy taxation of the clergy. Chapels were added to the choir of Notre-Dame by Pierre de Chelles and by Jean Ravy, who succeeded him in 1318. These two great architects also provided the apse with additional support by completing the flying buttresses that Pierre de Montereau had begun during the lifetime of Louis IX. Built of the hardest stone, leaping a full fifty feet in a single flight over the twin ambulatories to the top of the apse wall, these buttresses are truly wonderful achievements. The only one of the older flying buttresses remaining, the double-arched one nearest to the northern transept, emphasizes the grace and strength of the fourteenth-century work. The newer architects respected the work of their predecessors; they changed and supplemented it, but they did not tamper with its spirit.

Long before it was completed — in the first third of the fourteenth century — the cathedral of Notre-Dame de Paris had been playing a central role in the daily life of the city. Now, with its new wealth of chapels,

between fifty and a hundred masses a day could be said beneath its vaults. For there was a tremendous concentration of clerics living in the immediate vicinity of the cathedral, and many of them owed their "livings" — in the sense of prebends — to endowments for perpetual masses that went back centuries. Some of these clerics were housed in the sumptuous episcopal palace on the south side of the cathedral, some in the chapter's cloister and the various buildings for the church's administrative offices. In addition, the Île de la Cité saw a constant flow of visiting ecclesiastics from all over France, for priests considered it an honor to officiate in the great cathedral.

Paris was, in fact, assuming the character of a religious as well as a secular capital. In keeping with the growing national spirit — "nationalism" would be a misleading word for the attitudes of the fourteenth century — the French Church tended to augment its own organization. Frequent synods were held in Paris, and the meeting hall was Notre-Dame. There the assembled prelates deliberated on the pressing problems of the faith. They drew up edicts on the life of the clergy, the rules of excommunication, the maintenance of churches and cemeteries, the liturgy, and the administration of the sacraments. In ecclesiastical policy, Paris became the second capital of Christendom, and Notre-Dame often seemed more important than the Palace of the Popes at Avignon as an architectural symbol of authority.

And yet, for all the white- and red-robed prelates who bustled through the choir, Notre-Dame was very much the people's church. The pilgrimages that had been encouraged while it was still abuilding, to raise money,

persisted into later centuries. The faithful who lived in or around Paris — and this meant one-tenth the population of France — made a custom of paying an annual visit to Paris's church of Our Lady. The University of Paris, by then an institution a century old, with its own classrooms, residences, and government, did not forget its origins in the cathedral's theological schools. Once a year, students and masters paid a formal visit to the church on the Île de la Cité. Individual students came far more often to pray in the cathedral for success in their examinations and to leave testimonials to Mary when she helped them to pass. The sick came to pray for cures, and the prostitutes of the city — notably partial to Notre-Dame — flocked there, especially on Saturdays, to offer candles to the Virgin.

Innumerable processions began and ended at Notre-Dame. In times of public danger — when the Seine rose rapidly and flood threatened, during prolonged droughts, and during the pestilences that periodically ravaged city, country, and continent throughout so much of the fourteenth century — the costly shrines and reliquaries of crystal, gold, ivory, and enamel were brought out of the cathedral treasury. Chanting crowds followed the relics up and down the streets of Paris and then returned to Notre-Dame for further ceremonies.

Above all, throughout much of the fourteenth and fifteenth centuries, the people knelt countless times in Notre-Dame to pray for the success of the king's arms over the English enemy. For France and England were embroiled in that intolerable, interminable struggle that had become more a way of life than an armed conflict: the Hundred Years' War.

On November 9, 1422, a towering catafalque, tall as a man, with a canopy of cloth of gold on a vermilion ground and a blue border sown with gold fleurs-de-lis and rich embroidery, was carried across the Pont Notre-Dame and down the rue de la Juiverie to the cathedral of Notre-Dame. On the catafalque lay the effigy of a king, dressed in a mantle of cloth of gold trimmed with ermine and sable, the white-gloved hands holding a scepter and the rod of justice, a silver and gold crown upon the head. The people lined the streets or stood at their windows, men and women lamenting. All shops were closed, for the whole of Paris was in mourning.

Preceded by twenty-four heralds, the funeral procession passed with majestic deliberation through the streets. Behind the heralds came two hundred representatives of the poor of Paris, then the friars of the mendicant orders, the clergy of the collegiate churches, the canons of Notre-Dame and Sainte-Chapelle. All the latter walked in the right file; on the left came the students and faculty of the University of Paris. Then came the higher clergy, in black copes and white miters: the Bishop of Beauvais, the Bishop of Chartres, the abbots of Saint-Denis and Saint-Germain-des-Prés, and many others. The dignitaries of the state followed the clergy: the Provost of Paris bearing his mace, the king's chamberlains and valets, the equerries who took turns carrying the enormously heavy catafalque, the presidents of the Parlement of Paris.

Behind the bier, walking by himself in black mantle and cocked hat, came the man who had stage-managed this remarkably solemn funeral, and who more than all those other grave gentlemen represented the real power in Paris and much of France. The people stared coldly at him, for he was an Englishman: John of Lancaster, Duke of Bedford; third son of King Henry IV of England and brother of Henry V of England, who had died three months previously; Protector and Defender of the Realm; Regent of France; and uncle to the newly crowned King of England, the infant Henry VI, who was now heir to the throne of France as well.

A dreary century of wasting struggles between England and France, of civil wars in both countries, and economic distress and recurrent plagues, had brought the two exhausted nations to this temporary union. English possession of Aquitaine and claims to Normandy, the English alliance with Flanders and the French alliance with Scotland, the intermittent naval war between French and English shipmasters — these issues provided the fuel that kept the interminable war smoldering when it was not flaming. English dynastic claims to the throne of France, stemming from marital alliances that had been arranged in order to keep the peace, offered a pretext for reviving hostilities whenever the occasion seemed favorable to either side.

At Crécy in 1346 and at Poitiers a decade later, English arms had defeated the French with terrible efficiency. England won the battles, but the victors could not hold the territory of France. In the middle of the fourteenth century the Black Death ravaged both countries. And along with the ghastly mortality — in some cities a third and more of the population died — the plague brought a sense of doom and hopelessness. Revivalist religious fervor alternated with wild superstition. The behavior of the clergy (who often, from fear of contagion, refused victims of the disease the last

Invaded Nation, Divided Faith

rites) brought the Church into disrepute. New heretical movements gathered force. The frantic search for some explanation nourished that belief in witchcraft and those actual experiments in Satanism which fascinated and horrified Europe for centuries afterward. Tremendous economic and social changes followed as population declined, labor grew scarce, and the fields went untilled. But in the lulls between resurgences of the Black Death, which became endemic after 1350, the sporadic war between England and France went on and on.

In 1415 there seemed at last some prospect that the war would end, and end in England's favor. At Agincourt an army of hungry, wet, and tired Englishmen, led by King Henry V in person met fresh French troops in a narrow defile. Though outnumbered three to one, the English slaughtered some five thousand of the chivalry of France, who were trapped by the weight of their armor, and the stupidity of their military tactics. Thereafter, the English reconquered Normandy — battering down the walls of the cities with their new-fangled artillery — and overran most of France north of the Loire. By the treaty of Troyes Henry V was recognized as heir to the French throne, and to strengthen his claim he married Catherine, the daughter of mad King Charles VI of France. Henry's death in 1422, so shortly afterward followed by that of King Charles, left the infant Henry VI to inherit both thrones.

Charles, although insane for the greater part of his reign, had been king for forty-two years. When he died, one text tells us, "there were few who remembered how in times gone by kings of France had been borne to their graves, in what order the people should be ranged, each according to his estate, for the occasion was rare and nothing was committed to writing." That, at least, was the pretext for waiting nearly three weeks between the king's death and the actual funeral; and the long delay, in turn, made it essential to place an effigy rather than the king's body upon the catafalque. But in truth the court was paralyzed; nothing could be done until the Duke of Bedford returned from Rouen, where he was staying. Bedford promptly ended all discussions. The funeral of his brother was so recent that he had the course of such ceremonies clearly in mind, and he promptly dictated the form of the arrangements.

As the cortege approached Notre-Dame, all could see the two great banners with the royal arms that hung above the portals on the outside. Inside, the nave, choir, and all the pillars were covered from top to bottom with drapes stamped with fleurs-de-lis. The lower level was lighted by two rows of torches, the gallery by a vast array of candles whose weight — one pound each — the chroniclers dutifully noted.

A chapel had been constructed in the choir, the black hangings again bearing the royal arms. In each corner of the chapel stood an enormous, twenty-five-pound candle. The Duke of Bedford took the foremost seat in the choir, behind the statue of Our Lady. The chamberlains and a contingent of the members of Parlement sat on the same side. Near the altar were the bishops of Thérouanne and Chartres, the Rector of the University, and the canons. Vigils were sung, nine psalms and nine lessons, and then the company departed. At eight the following morning a requiem mass was celebrated, and then the whole funeral pro-

cession formed anew to follow the catafalque to Saint-Denis, where the actual body of Charles VI would be buried in its lead casket. Many of those who watched the procession must have been thinking sorrowfully that from now on the English House of Lancaster would sit on the throne of France.

Such might have been the case — and who can imagine what course the history of Europe might have taken — had it not been for the brief appearance of one of the most remarkable phenomena of the waning Middle Ages. In a meteoric career that lasted only two years a fervent seventeen-year-old girl from the little town of Domrémy revived the fading fortunes of the French monarchy and created the precondition for an independent and united France.

By his skillful conduct of affairs Bedford gradually reduced French hostility to the English occupation. As regent for Henry VI, Bedford governed his half of France with diplomacy and justice, observing local customs, and keeping those French officials who were willing to serve him. He expanded his domain toward the south, which was still controlled by the Dauphin Charles. Many Frenchmen were waiting impatiently for the as yet uncrowned Charles VII to claim his inheritance. But the shambling, knock-kneed "King of Bourges," as he was called — a man ashamed of his physical deficiencies, doubtful that he was a true son of the king, and too fearful to ride a horse across a bridge — made no move to oppose the English.

At this low ebb in the fortunes of France, the Maid of Lorraine emerged from her obscure country village. It is curious to reflect that Joan of Arc, who was to become the very symbol of French patriotism, was a

foreigner — for Lorraine was not then a part of France. She spoke *patois* most of the time, although she could manage correct and even eloquent French when she wished, for she was not a simple shepherdess but the daughter of a well-to-do farmer. But she and her fellow villagers believed in the cause of France and felt acute hostility toward the Burgundian allies of the English just across the River Meuse from Domrémy. Joan's hatred for the English sprang from more than romantic sympathy for poor Charles VII. English soldiers had burned her village, although her father's house, standing in the shadow of the church, was unharmed.

The miracle Joan wrought in the spirit of France, by her faith in her "voices," by her indomitable example on the battlefield, and by her martyr's death, would seem pure legend were it not amply attested to by historical documents. Joan inspired the dauphin by convincing him that he was not a bastard; she inspired the soldiers by her religious fervor combined with passionate nationalism; and she inspired the populace because she was the incarnation of their natural dislike for the foreigner. She had learned that Saint Remy, patron saint of her village church, had crowned Clovis the first King of France, and that this was the reason Reims was so closely associated with the royal line. And so, after her military victories, she dragged a reluctant Charles VII to his coronation at Reims in 1429. The king's anointment there made him legitimate in her eyes — and the common people of France held the same belief. After that coronation, the position of Charles VII was assured — and he himself lost his doubts about his own royalty.

Bedford tried to counter the prestige Charles had

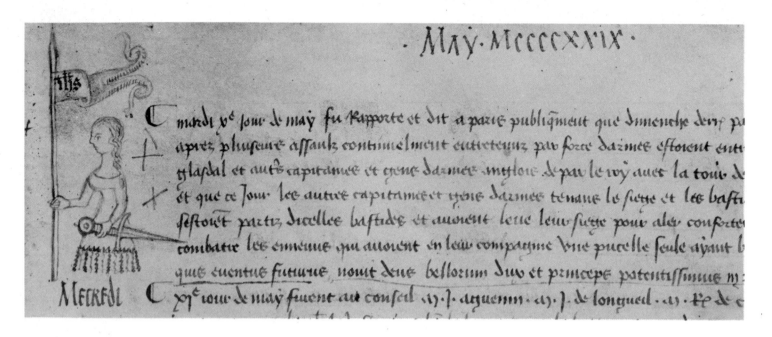

won by arranging a coronation of his own. He brought the young Henry VI to Paris, but he did not dare proceed with his plan until after Joan of Arc had been captured at Compiègne. Then, after Joan had been brutally disposed of, Bedford had Henry VI crowned in Notre-Dame de Paris on December 16, 1431. There was no tradition for such crownings at Paris, and nearly four hundred years were to pass before there was another: the coronation of Napoleon as emperor. And both were the coronations of usurpers who did not reign for long. Notre-Dame was the heart of France in other respects, but the French preferred to make their kings elsewhere. Even the ceremony for Henry VI's coronation "lacked dignity," we are told.

Joan had been captured by the Burgundians, but she was turned over to the English, who determined to ruin her character. With the aid of a collaborationist French clergy, and with what seems like the passive complicity of Charles VII, they convicted her of witchcraft and heresy, and Joan was burned at the stake. Charles displayed little gratitude for her services to him; he did nothing to ransom her or to save her from her fate. Apparently Joan made Charles uncomfortable; her whole personality reminded him of the deficiencies he had not yet overcome in those years of early, unwonted, and almost unwanted victories.

But then, ingratitude was to be the pattern of Charles VII's life. He was later called Charles the Well-Served, because so many of his successes could be attributed to his good counselors. One of these was another young girl, Agnès Sorel, whom Charles evidently found more to his liking than Joan because he could take her to his bed.

Charles dubbed Agnès "Madame de Beauté" — and she seems to have deserved the title. It is a measure of changing moralities after the Black Death that she became the first officially acknowledged royal mistress at a French court — first in a long and distinguished line. A level-headed, deeply religious young woman, concerned for the condition of the poor, she gave Charles good advice and reinforced his self-esteem. But her time at his side was short; his ardor cooled after a while and he failed to protect her against the intrigues of the court, just as he had failed to protect Joan. She died young, probably of poison.

It was Agnès Sorel, apparently, who persuaded Charles to advance the career of Jacques Coeur, one of the greatest of early medieval capitalists, who for a time put the finances and administration of France on a sound basis. As master of the mint Coeur reformed the debased French currency. As a merchant, he made an enormous fortune by establishing flourishing trade relations between France and the Near East. As a diplomat, he helped put an end to a papal schism. As a general, he both financed and helped direct Charles's successful war to drive the English from northern France. With his aid, Paris was taken, and on April 13, 1436, the great bells of Notre-Dame clanged to announce the entry of French troops into the city. Thereafter, a Te Deum was sung in Notre-Dame on every first Friday after Easter for 346 years, to celebrate the deliverance of the capital from the English occupation.

Shortly after the death of his mistress, Charles VII turned against his eminent adviser. Though there was no shadow of evidence or motive for such a crime, Jacques Coeur was accused of poisoning Agnès Sorel.

Coeur's enemies or debtors were appointed his judges; he was found guilty, all his wealth was confiscated, and in addition he was fined an enormous sum. After several years of imprisonment, he escaped to Rome, where he was warmly received at the papal court and appointed captain of an expedition against the Turks. But his privations and disappointment had been too much for him; he died in 1456, soon after beginning his second career.

Charles VII survived his great minister by only five years. But if the king's conduct toward Agnès Sorel and Jacques Coeur was singularly ignoble, Charles revealed a better side to his character when he initiated the rehabilitation trial of Joan of Arc. The Bishop of Paris, Guillaume Chantier, presided over this trial, whose sessions were held in the episcopal palace, by then larger and more magnificent than Maurice de Sully's original structure. Joan's mother figured officially as the plaintiff; many witnesses who had known and fought beside Joan of Arc gave vivid testimony; and in 1456 the condemnation of 1431 was declared null and void.

The movement Joan began had established France. By the time Charles died in 1461, nothing remained of the English holdings in France but the port of Calais. There was an underlying irony in the whole career of this weakling king who succeeded, far better than his dashing and bellicose predecessors, in driving the English from the soil of France. And the irony persisted even in his burial. Again forty years had passed between the deaths of kings, but this time good records had been kept. The obsequies for Charles VII followed in the main the pattern that had been established for the funeral of Charles VI. Once more Notre-Dame was draped in hangings stamped with fleurs-de-lis, such as had been ordered by the lifelong enemy of both Charleses, the Duke of Bedford.

During the lifetime of Charles VII the word Gothic first appears in the sense of something contemptible — not, however, in France, but in Italy. The universal genius Leon Battista Alberti, poet, painter, musician, architect, and writer on architecture, used the term in the sense of "rustic" or "boorish." Alberti also commented that the pointed arch did not exist in classical antiquity — which for a man of his time and temper was equivalent to saying that it ought not to exist at all.

Alberti was expressing a new spirit, a new fascination with the vestiges, the forms, the languages, and the literatures of classical antiquity. All that had been achieved in the thousand years between A.D. 410 — when Alaric's Goths sacked Rome — and "modern" times seemed an era of darkness perhaps briefly illuminated by the age of Charlemagne. Writers had employed a "barbarous" Latin so debased from the style of Cicero that a man of taste ought not to sully his mind with reading it. Sculptors had forgotten the beautiful forms of classical statuary and created stiff, unnatural poses or horrid, misshapen creatures like the ugly gargoyles on cathedrals. Architects had lost touch with rounded forms and the harmonious geometrical proportions of classical buildings. Infected by the barbarian tastes of the Gothic conquerors of Rome, they had gone in for fantastic turrets and spires, for all kinds of protuberances and excrescences. Thinkers had indulged in fruitless scholastic speculations on the nature of God and the number of the canonical virtues instead

of studying the operations of Nature. True wisdom had once been possessed by the Greeks, Chaldeans, Hebrews, Egyptians, and Romans; it had been lost during the long dark age in between, but men could still recover it if they would make the effort.

The new Humanists, as they called themselves, began an impassioned hunt for lost works of the ancient artists, sages, and poets. Financed by the merchant princes and bankers of the burgeoning Italian city-states, they ransacked the monasteries of Europe for manuscripts, and in this way they recovered for posterity many of the priceless works of the ancient world.

The recently invented art of printing helped them to spread their learning far and wide. Within fifty years of the publication of the first printed books in the middle of the fifteenth century, an estimated 20,000,000 copies of perhaps 40,000 different books had been printed. Erasmus of Rotterdam, the intellectual leader of the Humanists, for a time earned his livelihood as a printer's proofreader and editor. He preferred the freedom of hard work to the tempting offer of King Francis I of France, who was willing to pay Erasmus an enormous salary if he would assume direction of the newly founded Royal College of France.

Friend of kings and popes, courted by all the best minds of Europe, Erasmus possessed in the sixteenth century the moral and intellectual authority that Saint Bernard had enjoyed in the twelfth. And like Saint Bernard, he tried to reform the Church from within. Although he remained a loyal if scarcely ardent Catholic, his attacks on the clergy contributed to the atmosphere in which Protestantism sprang into being and throve. His editions of the Church Fathers, and his publication of a New Testament in the original Greek, provided the arsenal from which Martin Luther and his fellow reformers drew their weapons when they launched a frontal attack on the Roman Church.

Printing, as well as the venality of the sixteenth-century popes, had contributed largely to the scandalous increase in the sale of indulgences that Martin Luther denounced. Among the first products from Gutenberg's press had been beautifully printed indulgences; and by the first quarter of the sixteenth century these certifications for remission of sins were being turned out by the millions. Nor should we forget, since we are concerned here with the history of a cathedral, that the indulgence which brought on Luther's first dramatic act of rebellion had been issued to finance the building of Saint Peter's in Rome. This was the indulgence being distributed by Friar Tetzel when Luther challenged the whole practice by posting his Ninety-five Theses on the door of the church at Wittenberg.

The Reformation thus initiated was carried into France by the disciples of John Calvin, a former student at the Royal College. Calvin was French by birth, austerely logical by predilection, severe and moralistic because deeply convinced of man's corruptness and God's goodness. He was an effective speaker and gifted organizer, and his doctrines of predestination and lay control of the church spread rapidly among Frenchmen. The Huguenots, as the French Calvinists were called — presumably from the Swiss word *Eidgenossen,* or confederates — flourished especially in the old home of the Catharist heresy, the south of France. There the ancient antagonism to the Catholic Church had con-

Religious ferment was rampant on the Continent during the sixteenth century. In 1517 the German monk Martin Luther — seen preaching at far left — inaugurated the Reformation by posting his Ninety-five Theses condemning papal corruption. His influence spread rapidly, inspiring scenes such as the one at left in which rioters topple sacred images from a church. In England, the leader of the break with Catholicism was the king himself, Henry VIII. In the painting below, Henry rides to the Field of the Cloth of Gold, where he and Francis I of France feted one another, momentarily reviving more carefree days.

tinued to smolder like an underground fire for three centuries. It erupted violently and unpredictably.

Whenever Huguenots seized control of a town, they would drive out the bishop and strip the cathedral of its paintings and sculptures. During the disorders in Paris after the death of Francis I, they twice broke into the cathedral of Notre-Dame, smashed parts of the sanctuary screen, and knocked down the statue of the Virgin. But Paris remained resolutely Catholic throughout the disruptions of the civil and religious wars; each time the Virgin was devoutly replaced and repairs were begun on the screen.

Francis had brought the Renaissance to France; he had Leonardo da Vinci and Benvenuto Cellini in his employ for a while and tried to live with the magnificence of Italian Renaissance princes. The famous Field of the Cloth of Gold, where he and Henry VIII entertained one another and their enormous followings with tournaments and spectacles that went on for three weeks, accomplished nothing politically but provided matter for gossip for a whole generation — and cost a fortune. Francis ran through money so fast that one contemporary remarked: "He is well named after Saint Francis because he has holes in his hands."

But Francis I also left a dire heritage of hatred by his slaughter of the Vaudois Protestants at the end of his reign. And he had married his son, Henry II, to Catherine de Médicis, whose attempts to find a middle course between the struggling religious and political parties of France ended with her becoming one of the most execrated women in the country's history. Of the sons she bore Henry, three weaklings survived for a time, Francis II, Charles IX, and Henry III. During thirty years, while each lived out his short life and reign, Catherine tried vainly to master by intrigue the tottering monarchy of a distracted realm.

It was an age of strong women who sought with varying success to rule through men. In Paris, and indeed in Notre-Dame, began the tragic career of Mary Stuart, Queen of Scots. Mary was not yet sixteen; she had been betrothed to the Dauphin Francis for ten years and had been raised in France by the family of her uncle, the powerful Duke of Guise, the great chief of the Catholic party. On April 24, 1558, the wedding of Mary and Francis was celebrated in Notre-Dame with all the éclat due to such a great union. The French regarded Mary Stuart as heiress to the throne of England as well as Scotland, for Catholics considered Elizabeth illegitimate.

In keeping with the taste of the time, what was by then regarded as a gloomy old Gothic cathedral — Notre-Dame had reached the venerable age of four hundred years — was decorated à l'antique, in a Renaissance conception of the splendors of imperial Rome. The society reporters of the time tell us that the Duke of Guise arrived in grand style, followed by musicians. Then came a hundred Gentlemen of the King's Household, followed by the royal princes "so richly adorned and dressed that it was a marvelous thing." The Queen of Scots wore a dress white as lilies, "so richly and sumptuously made that it would be impossible to describe." Her necklace of precious stones was as dazzling as her golden crown, set with pearls, diamonds, rubies, sapphires, and emeralds, with an enormous carbuncle in the center.

As King Henry II and the Bishop of Paris entered

the cathedral, the heralds cried three times: "Largesse!" They began scattering gold and silver coins among the crowd, evoking such a tumult that it sounded like thunder. King Henry, Queen Catherine de Médicis, the dauphin, and Mary Stuart took their places under a canopy of cloth of gold, and when they knelt their knees rested on cushions covered with the same material. The Cardinal de Bourbon pronounced the nuptials, and the Bishop of Paris celebrated the mass.

The next year the Queen of Scots had become Queen of France, for Henry II was killed in a tournament, and young Francis succeeded him. Francis II doted on his beautiful wife, and during his brief reign the Guises worked their will in France. At the castle of Amboise, where Leonardo da Vinci had died, Francis and Mary sat in the royal garden overlooking the Loire watching while some twelve hundred Huguenots were led to the scaffold for participation in a plot to undermine the power of the Guises. In vain the queen mother urged moderation. Francis would listen only to Mary, and young Queen Mary was in all things obedient to her uncle, the Duke of Guise.

Only another year passed before Notre-Dame was once more draped, this time entirely in black, for the impressive funeral of Francis II. Nine months later his widowed queen, as resolute as she was beautiful, sailed for Scotland to claim her inheritance. For the next twenty-five years, until she too ended on the scaffold, her tangled loves and intrigues helped shape the history of Scotland and England, and often influenced the politics of France. French Catholics under the Duke of Guise supported her, while the French Huguenots frequently turned to Queen Elizabeth for aid during the many crises of the bitter religious wars in France.

Throughout those years of strife, while Elizabeth reigned in England and Mary spent much of her life a helpless captive, Catherine de Médicis attempted to govern France. Although a Catholic too, she nevertheless wanted to fend off the domination of the Guises, and so she strove to hold the balance between Huguenots and Catholics. But the factional passions were too strong for her diplomacy, and when she saw her second son, Charles IX, falling under the influence of the Huguenot Gaspard de Coligny, she repented her policy of conciliation. After Charles insisted on the marriage of his sister Marguerite to Henry of Bourbon, King of Navarre, one of the chiefs of the Huguenot party, Catherine conceived the horrible act of treachery with which her name will be forever associated.

Thousands of Huguenots had come to Paris for the wedding, and feeling was running high among the Catholics of the capital. A dais was erected on the parvis of Notre-Dame, and there the marriage ceremony was performed. Then Henry entered the cathedral with his bride, but before mass began he conspicuously withdrew to the garden of the bishop's palace. Three days of balls and tournaments followed to celebrate this first royal "mixed marriage," which was intended to unite Huguenots and Catholics.

Within a week of the wedding, Catherine had persuaded her son that a great Huguenot conspiracy was brewing and that if the Huguenots were not wiped out the cause of Catholicism in France would be lost. Unwillingly, so it is said, Charles consented to the demands of his mother and the Guises. At two o'clock in the morning on Sunday, Saint Bartholomew's Day—

dered the bodies burned and the ashes scattered, lest the Catholic party collect the bones of the Guises as relics. Six months later Henry III himself was stabbed to death by a fanatical Dominican friar, who thus put an end, in 1589, to the Valois dynasty. The young friar was instantly cut down by the king's guards; had he lived, he would have been appalled by the consequences of his brutal act. For the legal heir to the throne of France was none other than the heretical Henry of Navarre.

Henry IV understood that his task was to heal the wounds of division within the country. He had to fight for the succession against the Catholic party, and his most loyal supporters were of course Huguenots. For four years, therefore, he remained a Huguenot while gradually consolidating his position. But the majority of his people were Catholic, and Paris above all would not admit a Protestant king within its gates. Whether or not Henry ever said "Paris is worth a mass," he acted according to that precept. He abjured Calvinism, and in February 1594 he rode triumphantly into Paris, surrounded by his soldiers, and entered Notre-Dame to attend mass and a Te Deum. This time he did not withdraw to the bishop's garden when the mass began.

Henry's abjuration of Protestantism had naturally alarmed his former supporters. To reassure them, he issued the Edict of Nantes in 1598, guaranteeing freedom of worship for Huguenots wherever they were already established, granting them the same civil rights as Catholics, and allowing them to maintain garrisons in about a hundred fortified towns. For the time being, the Edict cooled if it did not settle the religious controversy, and Henry was able to proceed to the eco-

nomic and social reconstruction of a wracked France. He reorganized the judicial system, stimulated manufacturing, improved the condition of the peasantry, and altogether so restored prosperity and peace that he made himself the most popular of French kings since Saint Louis.

Witty, tolerant, generous, this first king of the Bourbon line found an able and intelligent Huguenot minister in the Duke of Sully, who contrived to put order into the catastrophic finances of France. Henry made his own contribution to financial and dynastic security by divorcing Marguerite of Valois, who had given him no heirs, and marrying Marie de Médicis, the pope's niece, who brought him an enormous dowry as well as children. But the old Catholic suspicions of the Huguenots would not die, and in 1610 the well-loved king was assassinated.

At Fontainebleau in 1608 an English traveler had seen Henry IV's seven-year-old son Louis, the "Dolphin whose face was full and fat-cheeked, his hair black, his look vigorous and courageous." At the age of nine this "Dolphin" succeeded to the throne; his mother, Marie de Médicis, became regent; and the nobles, whom Henry IV had kept under control, now became strong enough to raid the royal treasury.

From prosperity France plunged to the brink of financial ruin once more, and the Estates General was summoned to vote new taxes. It met in 1614 — for the last time before the French Revolution — but did little more than present a picture of a country once more rent by internal strife and on the verge of civil war. At the age of sixteen Louis XIII tried to shake off his mother's regency and rule alone, but he soon fell un-

der the domination of Cardinal Richelieu, that most worldly of ecclesiastics. If Henry IV had laid the foundations of French absolutism, Richelieu built the superstructure. He humiliated the nobles, drove the queen mother into exile, made foreign conquests, and frustrated incessant conspiracies. Louis XIII sporadically tried to gather the reins into his own hands, but most of the time he contented himself with a passive role. In the end he became so dependent on Richelieu that he outlived his mentor by only a few months.

In 1622, two months after Richelieu received his cardinal's hat, Pope Gregory XV made Paris an archdiocese, independent of Sens at last. The bishops of Meaux, Chartres, Orléans, and Blois became suffragans of Jean François de Gondi, the first Archbishop of Paris. Gondi continued in office for thirty-two years, and was succeeded by his nephew, the Cardinal de Retz, famous for his memoirs and for his prominent part in the conspiracy of the Fronde.

Louis XIII, the son of a Huguenot, was always subject to suspicions about the genuineness of his Catholicism — suspicions that drew sustenance from the foreign policies of Richelieu, who supported the Protestant princes of Germany in their struggle with the Austro-Spanish Habsburgs. Consequently, Louis took every opportunity to stress his orthodoxy. During his reign some forty religious houses were built in Paris, and some twenty churches begun. Early in 1626 three miraculous cures before the altar of the Virgin at Notre-Dame de Paris prompted Louis and his queen, Anne of Austria, to make a gift of a new altar for the Virgin's chapel in the cathedral.

Here was a longed-for chance to embellish the "bar-

VI Notre-Dame in Eclipse

Louis XIII's vow to build a new high altar for Notre-Dame was eventually fulfilled three quarters of a century after he had made it, by the son who had scarcely known him. For Louis XIV, who had so pertly announced his imminent accession when he was not yet five years old, sat on the throne for seventy-two years — the longest reign in the history of Europe. It was also the reign during which France became the greatest power in Europe, in which French virtually replaced Latin as the language of international diplomacy, in which French culture and manners were universally admired and imitated, French wealth envied, a French colonial empire founded, the French realm enlarged, a French civil service elaborated. Under Louis XIV Descartes and Pascal dominated mathematics, philosophy, and theology; Vauban, military fortification; Turenne and Condé, military tactics; Colbert, economic theory and practice — much as the French armies dominated Europe. A host of great French writers were read not only in France but throughout the civilized world. If French painters could not compare with their Italian and Dutch contemporaries, French interior decoration, furniture, and architecture had no rivals. Every king in Europe who had the means tried to imitate the vast halls and ornate glitter of the palace at Versailles. It was only fitting that a king who so dominated his age and his country should close his reign by trying to remake in his own image the solid Gothic structure of Notre-Dame.

The great reign began inauspiciously. As so often happened when a child inherited the throne, long-repressed frustrations erupted. By custom, France barred women from the succession but allowed queen mothers to exercise regencies during the minorities of their sons. And so Anne of Austria joined the long line of female regents that stretched from Blanche of Castile through Catherine de Médicis and Marie de Médicis. Like many of her predecessors in office, she was able to control the turbulent nobles only through bribery. *"La reine est si bonne"* — "The queen is so kind" — the courtiers murmured as they lined their pockets; and meanwhile they continued to conspire against the foreign cardinal Jules Mazarin, who succeeded Richelieu. The kind queen shared her bed as well as her power with Mazarin, who manipulated the factions as skillfully as he did his royal mistress. His informers were everywhere; he anticipated the moves of his enemies, who were also everywhere; and although he could not prevent the uprising of the Fronde (named after the slingshots with which the youth of Paris attacked the royal guards), he slid, slithered, and ducked as if running the gauntlet, and emerged triumphant at the end.

The Fronde, with its multiple treasons and rapid changes of sides by the magnates of France, was half comic opera, half an earnest dress rehearsal for the Revolution 140 years later. Mazarin, desperately in need of funds for himself, his bribes, and the armies that France was maintaining during the closing days of the Thirty Years' War, had attempted to impose a tax on all goods entering Paris. The Parlement of Paris, which like French parliaments of other cities was essentially a court of law, attempted to claim the powers its English namesake was then winning. It asserted wider authority than it had and refused to accept the tax. Mazarin and Anne, infuriated, waited for an opportunity to enforce their will. With the Prince of

Condé's notable victory over the Spaniards at Lens, in northern France, the moment seemed to have come.

On August 26, 1648, this victory was celebrated by a Te Deum in Notre-Dame. Seventy-three captured flags waved over the heads of the Parisians — whose leading representatives in the Parlement were at that moment being arrested. When someone saw a councillor being dragged into a carriage, popular indignation exploded. Barricades were thrown up in the streets of Paris. Jean François Paul de Gondi, coadjutor to the Archbishop of Paris (and the future Cardinal de Retz), hastened to court and pleaded for the councillor's release. When he was rudely rebuffed, he placed himself at the head of the rebels.

The students and sons of the middle class led the way in the street fighting and in writing scorching pamphlets called *mazarinades,* which attacked the prime minister, the court, and the nobility. But the lower classes likewise enthusiastically joined the citizens' army, whose major success was the capture of the Bastille. The court fled from Paris. To Anne of Austria, to eleven-year-old Louis XIV, the world seemed to be going mad. There were revolutions in Catalonia and Portugal, and in England a king — Charles I — had actually gone to the execution block. It would have taken a hardy prophet to predict, at the midpoint of the seventeenth century, that the next fifty years would witness the triumph of absolute monarchy on a scale unprecedented in the history of Europe.

The disorders in France continued for four years. At one point the regent, king, and cardinal were all forcibly detained in Paris, and in a scene to be repeated in the later great Revolution the Paris mob broke into the Louvre demanding proof that the king was still there. Anne was compelled to lead a delegation of Parisians into the boy-king's bedroom and to exchange friendly words with the *canaille.* Matters apparently grew even worse when the great nobles, led by the generals Condé and Turenne, took up the cause of the Fronde on their own behalf.

Mazarin, however, skillfully played on the patriotism of the bourgeoisie; he won over the Parlement by showing that the generals were making common cause with foreign enemies. Then he undermined the alliance between the Catholic Condé and the Huguenot Turenne, and took Turenne back into the royal service. Ultimately, the nobles themselves recognized that the monarchy was the sole stabilizing factor in the country, and they abandoned their opposition. But Louis XIV never forgot the humiliations he underwent during the period of the Fronde. Out of that experience sprang his lifelong distaste for the city of Paris and his determination to reduce the nobility to impotent courtiers and to keep the Parlement within its proper bounds as a legal tribunal.

The cardinal and the king emerged stronger than ever from the rebellion of the Fronde, though Louis remained under Mazarin's tutelage until the cardinal died in 1661. Then the twenty-three-year-old king announced that henceforth he would rule in his own right. His ministers smiled to themselves; surely in a week or two His Majesty would be bored and leave affairs to them. But they soon found that the king was in earnest. Moreover, he really worked at the task of governing. Although he had received a shamefully poor education, Louis had learned something from watching

rays in all di
sentations of
trade, and a
style fashiona
redecoration

France gre
tious wars an
No limit wa
for grandeur
In addition,
the capital.
eval Paris co
mous, still u
squares creat
those of anc
conceived th
serving as a
became the
proved to be
numerous wa

France wa
penditures,
Louis's grea
creased. But
upon the pe
bourgeoisie
the system o
to middleme
increased ar
upon those
Edict of Na
the Huguen
ing, capable

trousseaux, the king and queen provided money for the young couples to set up their households and dowries of five hundred livres for each of the girls.

This action was rather characteristic. Louis XVI was a man of simple tastes, personally kindhearted and virtuous, in striking contrast to his profligate predecessors. He was even a Freemason and a reader of the Encyclopédistes. As for his wife, the pretty, pampered Austrian princess was a disciple of the late Jean Jacques Rousseau. At her model farm in the park of Versailles Marie Antoinette and her court ladies played at the simple life. Louis, too, preferred hunting or his hobby of locksmithing to forcing through the fundamental reforms then generally known to be necessary. Whatever measures he did take turned out to be unfortunate. The privileged classes stubbornly resisted giving up any of their privileges or allowing the Third Estate an equal voice in public affairs. It was thus inevitable that the assembly of the Estates General, called at last by an unwilling king, should have reached an impasse.

When, in those July days of 1789, the common people of Paris emerged from their wretched quarters to listen to the inflammatory speeches of such youthful radicals as Camille Desmoulins and Georges Danton, they were hardly showing solidarity with the delegates of the Third Estate at Versailles who were defying the king's order to disband. Rather, the people poured into the streets from impatience with promises made and never kept, from indignation at the luxuries of the nobility, and from fear — which was to be the motive force for the excesses of the years to come. For word spread that there would be a Saint Bartholomew's Day massacre of liberals. Rumors flew that the Swiss and

German troops in the capital would be set upon the populace. The mob coursed through Paris, seizing arms. When it stormed the Bastille, it was attacking a symbol more than an actuality. The grim old fort, once part of the city's defenses, was already slated for demolition. In its place was to stand a statue of the enlightened and kindly Louis XVI, who was already doing away with past wrongs.

The Bastille, of course, was intimately associated with repressions and persecutions. Thousands of Huguenots, political troublemakers, pamphleteers, and others guilty of spreading seditious doctrines had been imprisoned there. There were also memories of the Fronde. In 1789 the Bastille fell easily. After the first few days of riot and bloodshed, the king took a conciliatory tone and promised the people a constitution. To celebrate the restoration of peace, a Te Deum was sung in the cathedral of Notre-Dame.

At its outset, the Revolution had scarcely any anti-clerical cast. In fact, les bons curés, the lesser clergy, were hailed as friends of the common people. With their help, the Church was to be cleansed of its corruptions and a better social order created. In those few weeks of strong emotion when all classes seemed united in recognition of the need for sacrifice, the Archbishop of Paris, Monseigneur de Juigny, set a personal example by donating 20,000 livres for the unemployed of the Saint-Antoine district. The canons of Notre-Dame made a gift of 12,000 livres. The people turned to their Church to sanctify their movement and asked to have the banners of their newly formed National Guard kept inside the cathedral. There was again a solemn ceremony in Notre-Dame, with the archbishop

blessing the banners. Further ceremonies of this sort were attended by the king and queen, and every effort was made to place the Church on the side of peaceful reforms.

But by October of 1789 the National Assembly, looking for suitable quarters, had installed itself inside the archiepiscopal palace. Monseigneur de Juigny began to feel uneasy and asked for a passport to leave the city and take the waters at Aix-les-Bains. Conditions were still stable in the south. The archbishop's departure was the signal for a general flight of the higher clergy. Within a few more weeks, a decree had been passed declaring all possessions of the Church the property of the nation.

The articles of precious metals in the cathedral's treasury were the first objects of this edict. Inventories were drawn up and receipts issued as reliquaries and chalices were delivered to the mint. But once the church had been stripped of its most conspicuous riches, an attack began on its larger holdings and prerogatives. The Chapter of Notre-Dame was dissolved, and the canons were forbidden to enter the cathedral. In November 1790 they celebrated their last mass. Religious establishments of every sort were banned and their buildings seized. The clergy were to be servants of the people, receiving fixed salaries, and they were required to sign a pledge of loyalty to the law, the king, and the nation.

About half the clerics accepted these conditions; they made up the so-called constitutional clergy. In March 1791 they met in the cathedral to elect an archbishop — to be known, since memories of the old hierarchy were to be suppressed, as the Metropolitan of the Seine.

The structure of the entire French Church was reorganized, the number of dioceses greatly reduced, and Notre-Dame designated as simply one parish church among others. It was now to serve for civil ceremonies as well as religious ones. Thus the anniversary celebration of the fall of the Bastille was held in the cathedral, with martial trumpet blasts and cymbals imitating the roar of cannon, while the chorus sang, "Down with the bastion of slavery." The performance, however, concluded with the traditional Te Deum.

Even such compromises could not quiet the growing spirit of anticlericalism. Among the flood of pamphlets and broadsides issued at the time were some that specialized in the most savage attacks on religion and the Church. This propaganda accorded with the general temper of militancy and panic. The new republic was barely proclaimed when it was fighting for its life against German regiments reinforced by troops of émigré nobles. In haste, a mass army was being formed. Arms, uniforms, and food were desperately needed, but the coffers of the new government were empty. Again the answer to the problem lay in the churches. Articles of bronze, tombs, monuments, choir grilles were carted off to be melted into cannon. Since those churches still authorized for worship were permitted only one bell, an inventory was made of the size and weight of the bells of Notre-Dame.

Each bell had a popular name and a well-known history. In the north tower hung Guillaume, a gift of Bishop Guillaume of Auvergne, dating back to the thirteenth century; Gabriel, a gift of Louis XI in 1477; Pugnese, Pasquier, Thibault, Jean, Claude, Nicholas, and Françoise. The south tower held Marie, a fifteenth-

society. After two years of negotiations with Pope Pius VII, he prepared to restore the Roman Catholic Church to its old dignity, if not to its old power.

The date set for the celebration of the Concordat was Easter Day, 1802. The prefect of the police made a hasty report on the condition of the cathedral. He found the inside fairly clean except for the chapels, which were boarded over with rough planks and had been robbed of flooring. These would have to be masked with tapestries, which fortunately were readily available at the Museum of National Monuments. There was even a suitable monstrance still at the mint. Desecrated, denuded, the cathedral was to be revivified and once more arrayed for a solemn Te Deum.

The *bourdon,* long absent from its loft, was hoisted back into its place. As the first rays of the April sun began to bathe the towers of Notre-Dame, the strong low notes of the bell rang out. Instantly, all the inhabitants of the nearby streets came to the windows. People on the streets embraced each other and wept. The consuls set out from the Tuileries, along with the ministers, councillors of state, and the members of the diplomatic corps seated in the old ornate royal carriages. Crowds lined the streets to look at the unwonted display. The first consul, Napoleon, in red uniform, was wildly applauded. The corps of soldiers that surrounded him, however, indulged themselves in shockingly antireligious remarks. The new Archbishop of Paris greeted the consuls at the west portal with the ceremonial used for royalty. They were accompanied to a dais set up facing the one on which the pope's emissary sat. Solemn addresses hailed the reestablishment of peace between France and her European enemies, a peace sealed by the restoration of religion.

Nevertheless, a certain cynicism was in the air. Emerging into the sunlit parvis filled with Parisians who had crowded about the cathedral in solid ranks, the first consul asked one of his generals what he had thought of the ceremony. The reply he made was quoted widely throughout Napoleon's entourage. "A fine show," the general said. "All that was lacking were the million or so men killed in order to destroy the thing which you have just reinstituted."

In August of that same year another plebiscite overwhelmingly confirmed the first consul's popularity. He was given the consulship for life, with the right to choose his successor. Two years later an unprecedented ceremony took place in Notre-Dame. Napoleon took the crown from the hands of Pius VII and crowned himself Emperor of the French. Monarchy was back, though under another name and with a different complexion. The old social order had been utterly smashed by the violence of the Revolution, but Napoleon fabricated a new one, which retained many of the reforms of republicanism, though within an authoritarian and centralized framework. His troops continued to win extraordinary victories and were greeted everywhere as liberators, freeing the people from outworn feudal regimes. Napoleon set his brothers and closest associates on the thrones of conquered kingdoms. France was truly an empire now, controlling the whole of Western Europe, and the coastline from Antwerp as far south as Genoa.

Napoleon's marriage to Joséphine, which dated from the time he was a mere officer, was without issue, and he had prudently left himself an opening for divorce.

Napoleon's evident determination and undeniable charisma — both suggested in the bas-relief study at left — help explain his meteoric rise to power. Only a man of such dynamism and self-assurance would have dared to assume the title Emperor of France a mere twelve years after the monarchy had been so overwhelmingly rejected. One of David's preliminary sketches (right above) for his panoramic coronation scene shows Napoleon placing the crown upon his own head, while a reproving Pius VII looks on. Another sketch (below), depicting the emperor's first wife, Joséphine, kneeling at her husband's feet to receive her own diadem, was incorporated in the final canvas (overleaf).

His second marriage, to the eighteen-year-old Archduchess Maria Louisa of Austria, perhaps marked the peak of his fortunes. The populace was treated to an elaborate show of fireworks above the cathedral of Notre-Dame, and a year later the cathedral was the scene of a magnificent baptism. The child's godfather was none other than Emperor Francis I of Austria, Maria Louisa's father, who was represented by one of his sons; the godmother was Napoleon's mother. An uncle of Napoleon, the Cardinal-Archbishop of Lyons, administered the sacraments. When the ritual was over, Napoleon took the baby from the arms of his attendants, kissed him heartily three times, and bestowed on him the title of King of Rome. The realm the child would have inherited was almost that of an emperor of the Romans.

In fact, he inherited nothing, and spent most of his short life at his grandfather's palace of Schoenbrunn in Vienna. He died at the age of twenty-one, thus sparing Europe what might have been a political embarrassment. For within a few years after his birth his father's star had waned. The record of fantastic victories turned into a series of defeats, and the Emperor of the French became General Bonaparte, a lonely prisoner of the English on a desolate island in the middle of the South Atlantic Ocean.

VII A Treasure Preserved

With the restoration of the Bourbons in 1814, the marble statues of Louis XIII and Louis XIV could once more enrich the sanctuary of Notre-Dame. The theatrical Descent from the Cross by Costeau had already been returned, on Napoleon's orders, to its place behind the high altar. But the other two figures of the ensemble, the kneeling kings, had been tactfully kept in the Museum of National Monuments until the time was ripe for their reappearance. Tact was in fact the keynote of the restored monarchy. The new king, Louis XVIII, was already sixty years old, afflicted with gout, and chastened by his long exile. He offered the country a constitution modeled closely on English lines and promised to recognize the results of the Revolution.

At the moment such common sense was precious. France had paid dearly for the years of Napoleonic glory. Her manpower had been exhausted by a quarter century of continual levies, so that the new monarchy's reforms in the conscription system were especially welcome. Louis XVIII managed to mitigate the harshness of the peace treaties. He also faced the long-term task of maintaining a balance between the two distinct and irreconcilable elements of French society — the émigrés and conservative interests on the one hand, the republicans and Bonapartists on the other.

Gradually, however, the government shifted to the right — freedoms were abridged, the press muzzled, the propertied class blatantly favored by changes in suffrage. When Charles X succeeded his brother in 1824, he made no secret of his impatience with constitutional processes. A series of confrontations between the king and the Chamber of Deputies ended with Charles X dissolving that body early in 1830. His troops were totally unprepared for the riots that erupted in Paris. Barricades sprang up and the king, who remembered 1789, thought it best to abdicate.

At the very outset of the rioting an assault was made on the archiepiscopal headquarters, Maurice de Sully's old palace, which flanked the cathedral on the south. A mob broke in and with lively memories of revolutionary tradition began to pillage and destroy whatever ecclesiastical goods they could find. A second attack on the palace, this time accompanied by arson, took place the following year. It would seem that the building, like the late unlamented Bastille, had a symbolic meaning for any insurrection. The cost of repairs would be great, and it was decided to raze the palace.

The site so long occupied by the archiepiscopal palace was converted to a broad promenade along the Seine. This was a democratic bit of civic improvement, in keeping with the character of the new head of state. Louis Philippe, the former Duke of Orléans, had been called in by the moderates after the abdication of Charles X. In the early stages of the Revolution, Louis Philippe had been a fervent advocate of republicanism, and now he studiously avoided the monarchical manners and reactionary policies that had been the downfall of his predecessor.

The cathedral, hemmed in from the beginning by a huddle of other buildings, more and more was standing in the clear. Everyone could now see how poor its condition was. Gothic structures had been little prized in the past several centuries — indeed, some ten medieval churches on the Île de la Cité alone had been demolished in various building programs, without the least regret on the score of their antiquity or artistic

value. But in 1830 a new feeling for the monuments of the past was arising. This was part of the romantic movement then sweeping Europe. Vast changes in the social fabric, whose extent could not yet be seen and whose implications could not be fathomed, produced a countercurrent: a passion for the strange, the faraway, the fantastic, the exalted, for richer forms of life than the banal present seemed to allow. Suddenly a building like Notre-Dame, so long taken for granted if not detested as an embodiment of superstition, was seen in a new light.

A rising young writer named Victor Hugo set the tone for this revaluation. In his *Notre-Dame de Paris,* published in 1831, he glorified architecture as living history; to Hugo a building was "a book in stone" — Gothic cathedrals in general and Notre-Dame in particular. Turning upon the eighteenth century, he denounced its refinements as silly fashion. He listed the indignities that had been wreaked on the cathedral of Paris in the name of so-called taste: its richly colored windows gone, its interior whitewashed, its flèche ripped off, the shape of the central portal mutilated, its chapels choked with showy rubbish, its choir floored with gaudy marble, its sanctuary cluttered with histrionic statuary.

Hugo's novel strongly influenced another young Parisian of talent, only seventeen at the time but already devoting himself to architecture. This was Eugène Emmanuel Viollet-le-Duc. The name was to become almost synonymous with restoration. While still in his early twenties, Viollet-le-Duc was appointed to the newly established commission for the preservation of historic monuments. For there was a movement

afoot, thanks largely to Hugo's novel, to save the buildings that represented the country's great past.

Prosper Mérimée, a man of letters best known to us as the author of the tale of Carmen, headed the commission. He took Viollet-le-Duc on a strenuous tour of the south, where they inspected a vast number of buildings, many dating from the eleventh century, which were in desperate disrepair. Soon Viollet-le-Duc was given charge of difficult projects. His ardor and competence were extraordinary, his capacity for work prodigious. The experience he accumulated from working on these projects gave him a staggering knowledge of Gothic and Romanesque building techniques. He could say at once what strategies were safe and what measures would be fatal to the intricate medieval balances. He drew up reliable estimates of costs and schedules. He organized building crews, trained craftsmen, promoted the growth of workshops — all this for as many as twenty projects at a time. He traveled continually, checking on reconstructions in progress and advising on those being considered. In 1845 he was appointed architect for the restoration of Notre-Dame de Paris. He was to be occupied with that task for the next twenty years.

Viollet-le-Duc had developed a philosophy of restoration. He was to state it again and again in his many writings, and above all in his vast study of French architecture, cast in the form of a dictionary that ran to ten volumes. But he expressed his principles early and clearly in his proposals for Notre-Dame:

In a project of this sort, one cannot proceed with enough prudence and discretion. A restoration can do more harm to a monument than the ravages of the

centuries and the fury of rioters. For time and revolution destroy but add nothing. A restoration, on the other hand, by adding new forms, can erase a host of details which are all the more interesting for being worn and rare. It is hard to say which is more dangerous — the indifference which lets buildings fall into total ruin or the ignorant zeal which shears away, adds on, carries to completion, and ends by transforming an ancient building into a new one, devoid of the slightest historical interest.

Yet he was not a purist. He appreciated the singularity of each building, which arose precisely from the span of time and range of styles it embodied. He was seeking an unspecific yet tangible quality of authenticity. To him the Gothic exemplified logic, honesty, lucidity, and function, and he preached these virtues for contemporary building too. Contrary to a popular misconception, which has equated his work with the archaizing pasticherie of the beaux arts tradition, Viollet-le-Duc should be considered one of the fathers of modernism. In addition to stressing the interdependence of form and function, he took great interest in the birth of such new architectural creations as railroad stations and market halls, in the possibilities of new materials such as cast iron, and even in the future of prefabrication.

Although he may first have fallen in love with the Gothic on romantic grounds, he came to admire it for its serviceable qualities. "Here are monuments which have lasted for six or seven hundred years, in spite of a destructive climate, in spite of three centuries of abandonment, in spite of fires and revolutions. Yet they are still in daily use, prove themselves convenient,

and need nothing but a little repairing, often no more than ordinary maintenance."

Viollet-le-Duc was keenly aware of the limits of restoration. The naïve spirit that had guided the original sculptor's chisel was dead and could not be willed into being again. Instead of creating new ornaments, he leaned heavily on archaeology and based his reconstructions on precedent. Thus he re-created the windows of Notre-Dame by copying other stained glass which had escaped destruction. It was he who enlisted the new techniques of chemistry for an analysis of the secrets of thirteenth-century glassmaking. To replace the sculptures of Notre-Dame smashed during the Revolution, he could draw on pictorial records and careful studies of the figures at Chartres, Reims, and Amiens. He designed the delicate wooden flèche to crown the crossing of the transept, the hinges of the great doors, the gargoyles of the rooftops. He had the inside of the cathedral scoured of its old whitewash and the outside treated with a silicone process to protect it from the atmospheric pollutants that were already a problem in nineteenth-century Paris. In addition, he built the sacristy adjoining the south side, needed for the cathedral's religious functions since it had lost its former annexes.

In this one portion of the building he was "Gothicizing," and the result has a charm all its own for our century. He also allowed himself such scholarly liberties as restoring some of the windows of the clerestory back to their twelfth-century form: smaller than the later windows and paired with blind roses. Since he filled these windows with clear rather than colored glass, they gave the interior a bit more light, welcome

Only seventeen when he sketched the sack of the archiepiscopal palace (far left) behind Notre-Dame in 1831 — and only three years older when Monvoisin executed his portrait (near left) — Eugène Emmanuel Viollet-le-Duc was destined to oversee the triumphant restoration of the cathedral of Paris. During the two decades he devoted to "Gothicizing" Notre-Dame, Viollet-le-Duc supervised the demolition of many of the crumbling structures (right) that hemmed in the cathedral — a task that continued after the architect's death in 1879.

to our modern taste. They also make an interesting historical point. He had endless decisions to make, for the cathedral incorporated a great many styles, not one of which could be considered definitive. He himself was biased toward a certain ascetic bareness, particularly where the chapels were concerned, and he has been somewhat criticized for this. But he relented in regard to the high altar built to fulfill the vow of Louis XIII. "It would be a shame to destroy a thing of such luxurious and tasteful workmanship and put in its place something of which we have only a few vague descriptions."

Restoring Notre-Dame was an enormous task. Viollet-le-Duc repaired the structure literally from the foundations to the tiling of the roofs. As he explained in his report, it was only in taking the work in hand that he saw how grave the cathedral's troubles were, the essential nature of what had to be done, and the danger of half measures. His diagnoses and remedies have proved their soundness. Notre-Dame stands substantially as he left it in 1864. Although he ran through more than one allocation, new funds were always voted for him. Building in France no longer depended on the whim of kings but on sober-minded deputies — yet they proved remarkably generous toward the cause of restoration.

Nevertheless, the country was undergoing severe economic strains. The crisis of 1848, marked by a stock exchange crash, unemployment, hunger, and workers' uprisings bloodily suppressed, brought to the fore an unlikely figure. This was Charles Louis Napoleon Bonaparte, third son of Napoleon's brother Louis. In the turbulence that swept away the citizen-king Louis

Philippe, he came forward as the heir to Napoleon, representing order, authority, religion, and concern for popular welfare. For a few years Louis Napoleon was President of the Republic. As such, he systematically suppressed all opposition forces and used the machinery of government to eliminate constitutional checks on his power. By 1852 he had the title he had long coveted: emperor.

The following year the cathedral of Notre-Dame, though not too far along in its refurbishment, saw the last of France's royal weddings. Napoleon III's bride was a titled Spanish girl, Eugénie de Montijo. Her striking beauty, her feeling for elegance, and her charm were to leave their stamp on the era. The outward brilliance of the Second Empire was to a large extent identified with Eugénie.

Viollet-le-Duc was commissioned to plan the wedding decorations for the cathedral. His design was a triumph of showmanship, and in its superabundance the very epitome of the regime's style. A pavilion was erected in front of the western façade, its panels painted in the manner of tapestries with representations of the saints and ancient kings of France. Vast figures of Charlemagne and Napoleon were fixed to the two main piers of the façade. The balustrade above the Gallery of Kings was decked with eagles and garlands. Nine green banners embroidered with Napoleonic bees and the imperial insignia waved above that. The higher levels of the façade were lost behind the flags of the eighty-six departments of France, more green streamers decorated with bees, vast standards of eagles, canopies of cloth of gold, and — topping each tower — an enormous tricolor flag.

For a while the country seemed prosperous and all went well for the imperial couple. A son was born to them and was baptized in the cathedral in the presence of no fewer than eighty-five high church dignitaries. Viollet-le-Duc was asked to design a great font for the ceremony, something in Byzantine style to be made out of Sèvres porcelain. He answered dryly that there was a copper vessel in the Louvre which had been used for the baptism of Saint Louis's children and should do perfectly well in this case. The suggestion was accepted, although in other respects there was no stinting of expense. Four new bells were installed in the towers and rung for the first time on this fourteenth of June 1856. The day before, Viollet-le-Duc was asked to make a personal search of the cathedral cellars — the architect knew them so well — as a security check.

Acts of terrorism had become common all through Europe, and a deep nervousness had begun to pervade the Second Empire. Louis Napoleon saw his popularity waning and attempted to win it back by making long-promised concessions to constitutional freedom. Then in a desperate desire to show strength, he provoked a war with Prussia in 1870.

Viollet-le-Duc was climbing in the Alps when news of the declaration of war reached him. His forebodings were expressed in a letter to his son: "Even if this war will not be a long one, it cannot be other than terrible." Although already fifty-six, he returned quickly to Paris and threw himself into the improvised defense effort there. The news from the front was bad, and soon it became worse. In a month the French forces were outflanked and large numbers taken prisoner, including the emperor himself.

With the Prussians on French soil, the patriotism of Paris rose to great heights. "We are in a pretty mess," Viollet-le-Duc wrote. But he praised the spirit of his outfit, made up of architects and workers in the building trades, almost all of whom he knew. With the Prussians on their way to encircle the city, he and his men were dispatched to Saint-Denis to take hasty measures to protect the edifice. He had scaffolding set up and sandbags piled, but the heavy Prussian bombardment severely damaged the abbey church. Some of the oldest stained glass in France was smashed.

War plays tricks on concepts of morality. In Paris, too, such tricks were being played. Cut off from food and fuel, with all normal functioning halted, the city abounded in terrible sights. Typhus broke out. There were many deaths from general privation. The poor, with nothing to sell or pawn, had the worst of it, but apparently their will to resist continued strong. In the rest of France there was one party that favored making peace, another for holding out against the harsh Prussian terms. A monarchist assembly had been elected, but it inspired little confidence. The National Guard, holding Paris against the encircling Prussians, was largely made up of the working class. When the legal government finally capitulated — Prussia's price was an indemnity of five billion francs, the cession of Alsace and Lorraine, and a long period of occupation — these contingents refused to give up their arms. Faced with revolution, the government fled to Versailles. The insurgents ran up the red flag over the Hôtel de Ville and proclaimed a people's government, the Commune.

Karl Marx, writing an account of the experiment only a few days after it was over, described the Com-

mune as a self-controlled, courageous venture run on the highest moral principles, and able — in the ten weeks at its disposal — to create a host of viable institutions. He saw Louis Napoleon's war and all that followed as a complicated plot on the part of the ruling classes to crush the rising power of the workers. The rest of France, he maintained, would soon have risen and made the revolution general. These interpretations were consonant with his larger theories on the historical inevitability of revolution. Whatever the case, in the last days of May 1871 the Versailles troops broke into the city. They had to win it street by street.

In the cathedral of Notre-Dame there is a black marble plaque commemorating sixty-three hostages shot by the Commune, among them the archbishop and five other ecclesiastics. The plaque tells only one side of the story. It would be only fair to tell the other side. The Communards had repeatedly asked for the release of their leaders. The hostages were being held as guarantees for the lives of these leaders, and the shootings took place only when the Bloody Week — as the days of May 21 to 28 were henceforth known — began. The government forces remained confident of eventual victory and obdurately refused to exchange prisoners. When the city fell and the government troops moved in to restore order, they rounded up all who could be suspected of taking part in the defense of the Commune. At least 20,000 persons, including women and mere boys, were mowed down by the *mitrailleuse,* the primitive machine-gun introduced into the French army just before the war. These victims of martial law were executed without even the pretense of a trial. There were also many more "legal" victims. For years

afterward trials continued and sentences of death or transportation to the colonies were meted out to the survivors of the massacre.

"I passed my day looking at Paris burn. It is a dead, destroyed, and annihilated city," the novelist Ludovic Halévy wrote of May 24, 1871. But seventeen days later, he reconsidered. "It is still the most beautiful city in Europe, and the most brilliant, and the most gay."

With so many painters setting up easels in the open air — according to the decree of Impressionism — it was inevitable that the cathedral should become a favorite subject of artists in the succeeding Third Republic. Much painted, much sketched, much etched and, with increasing interest in the camera, much photographed, Notre-Dame became an ever more familiar image to those who might not actually set eyes upon her. To local inhabitants she was more visible than before, as several more buildings around her were razed. Admirers of the medieval might criticize the change and point out that widening the vista detracted from the effect of the façade. But there was surely something to be said for the sunny park, the bright parterres, and the softening line of trees that took the place of the Hôtel Dieu, that ancient, insalubrious hospital, and the equally obsolete foundling home.

This new fringe of green about the gray old edifice, where children played and lovers met, where the old enjoyed the sun and tourists collected their strength, represented still another face that Paris disclosed to the twentieth century. Paris was the City of Light, of heightened sensibility, of seasoned beauty, of humane tolerance and worldly wisdom, of faith and skepticism, of artistic audacity, and of intellectual rigor. It was

dense with tradition yet receptive to the new. No wonder Paris was the mecca for aspiring artists from all of France, all of Europe, all the world. Everyone who came, whether to visit or to stay, paid his respects to the cathedral. Notre-Dame was the soul of the city.

The uses of the cathedral had changed somewhat; it had a new part to play in the life of the nation. For in the twentieth century the nature of ceremony had altered. There were still great formal rites set in Notre-Dame, but these were no longer hierarchic, revolving about the fortunes of royalty, their weddings, baptisms, and funerals. The Third Republic, born with such pangs, proved remarkably durable. The ceremonies of a republic are apt to be lacking in color, but perhaps make up for this by wider and more genuine participation. Their real theme is the survival of the nation.

The ceremonies for the beatification of Joan of Arc were no exception to this rule. These took place in Notre-Dame in 1909 and evoked an outpouring of emotion all over France. Not only did this inspired, fearless, and unconventional girl correspond to a new ideal of femininity emerging at this time, but she was also the Maid of Lorraine. Forty years had passed since the short, disastrous war in which that province had been forfeited, but the loss still rankled. Joan had rallied the French to expel the foreign invader and recapture lost territories. It was timely indeed that she was now numbered among the blessed.

By that year the enemy was no longer the English, but those offensively successful Germans. Their disparate states were unified into an empire whose interests crossed with those of France in more than one sector. The Kaiser rattled his saber in a manner that

other European nations found hard to bear. Alliances formed. England, France, and Russia discovered a common bond, while on the other side were ranged Germany, Austria-Hungary, and that once formidable but now crumbling Moslem power, the Ottoman Empire.

The Great War came in 1914. The German general staff had envisaged it as another quick thrust. They attacked through Belgium and almost reached Paris, but the resolute stand of British, Belgian, and French troops checked their impetus. There were fresh advances and breakthroughs, then stalemate. This was an unprecedented form of warfare with new rules and new weapons. Tanks were used, as were long-range artillery and the small, fragile airplanes that opened possibilities for destruction so far undreamed of. Science provided another innovation: poison gas.

Strangely enough, all sides had gone to the battlefield in a mood of patriotic exaltation and readiness for sacrifice. But the slaughter on both sides was ghastly; the euphoria wore off as the ordeal dragged on. Russia fell away, victim of defeat and internal revolution. In 1917 a fresh and jaunty army of Americans arrived.

All through the war, prayers had been said in the cathedral for France and her armies. Once more the ancient relics, whose efficacy would seem to have dwindled in modern times, were brought out and carried in procession down the aisles of Notre-Dame. Paris was spared the worst blows of the war, although the first small shells fell upon her as early as September 1914. In October of that same year one bomb penetrated the roof of Notre-Dame over the north transept, causing some damage. Other great Gothic monuments did not get off so lightly. Reims cathedral, where

French kings since Clovis had been crowned, was reduced to near ruin.

To hail the armistice of November 1918 there was a great Te Deum in Notre-Dame. The cathedral was filled to bursting. The decorations were all flags, the important personages generals, and the altar draped in the tricolor. The priest who said mass came from Alsace, once more a part of France. The score had been righted. This time it was the Germans who saw their empire dismembered. Moreover, they had to pay heavy indemnities for war guilt and surrender the iron-rich Saar to French occupation; they were also denied the right to an army. But the price had been staggering on both sides. This came to light over the next two decades in the insecurity of the social order, in economic collapse, and in the emergence of pathological creeds among the vanquished.

In both France and Germany commanding figures of the previous era passed away. In 1929 Notre-Dame was draped in black for the funeral of Marshal Foch, the Allied supreme commander of World War I. There was a somber ceremony before the casket was placed on a horse-drawn gun carriage waiting on the parvis before the cathedral. The cortege consisted of other eminent and aging generals who followed on foot as the procession made its way to the Arc de Triomphe, where the casket was set beside the tomb of the Unknown Soldier, to lie in state before burial at the Invalides. Thus public ritual paid homage to the innumerable *poilus* on whose sacrifices the reputations of the great ultimately rested.

This emphasis was natural for France, where the principles of Rousseau's *Social Contract* had become

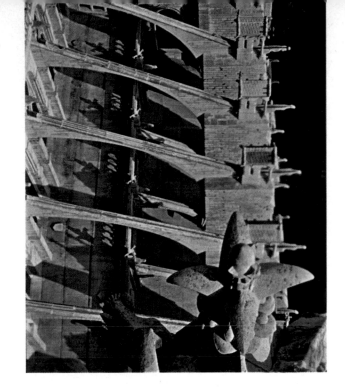

The massive bulk of the twin towers of Notre-Dame — seen at left from the southeast — is relieved by the presence of decorative finials and crockets. At right is an unusual view from above of the cathedral's famed flying buttresses.

assimilated into the national character. It was somewhat different in Germany. There General von Hindenburg, the German counterpart of Foch in the Great War, had been installed as president since 1925. Hindenburg, too, stood for the soldierly virtues. He was an authoritarian figure, still an honorable one, hewn on majestic nineteenth-century lines. His death in 1934 opened the way to absolute power on the part of an authoritarian figure of quite another sort: Adolf Hitler. A thwarted self-taught architect, a lowly corporal during the war who in the difficult postwar years joined the flotsam and jetsam of the big cities, Hitler conceived a mission for himself, came forth as a leader, and built up a heterogeneous party. He understood the grievances of the Germans and their crying need for simple answers and large promises. Germany's new chancellor unilaterally abrogated the humiliating peace terms of the treaty of Versailles, built an army, moved troops into prohibited areas, made outrageous demands — and found that they were granted. In France, all this was chiefly seen as the stirrings of the hated Boche. France strengthened her military defenses. The Maginot Line was considered impregnable.

When, after a deceptive lull, the Germans attacked France in May 1940, they again relied on the impetus of surprise. They parachuted troops behind the fortified lines and, coming through the Low Countries, outflanked the Maginot Line. They could also count on secret allies in the invaded regions. But even more significant than outright treachery was the general mood of fatalism in France. Many responsible people, including large portions of the officer corps, saw little hope in holding off this onslaught. The previous war

was too recent, its toll too well remembered. Within five weeks German troops were occupying Paris.

Hitler himself came to see his prize. He made a sightseeing tour, surely one of the most bizarre ever undertaken. It began at five-thirty in the morning and was over by nine. Hitler knew what he wanted to see: the Opéra, the Trocadero, the Eiffel Tower, the Arc de Triomphe, and the Invalides, where he stood for a long time by the tomb of Napoleon. He admired the Pantheon and had himself driven to Montmartre to see the church of Sacré-Coeur. Notre-Dame was not on his itinerary.

That same evening, back in his command post, Hitler gave orders reactivating his ambitious plans for the rebuilding of Berlin. "Wasn't Paris beautiful?" he said. "But Berlin must be made far more beautiful. In the past I have often considered whether we would not have to destroy Paris. But when we are finished in Berlin, Paris will be only a shadow. So why should we destroy it?"

France, divided into the occupied territory and the so-called Free Zone, lived for the next four years at the mercy of such caprices. In the first days of the war, measures had been taken to protect the cathedral. The rose windows were removed, the portals blocked with sandbags. After the Germans had entered the city, the bells remained silent. On the first anniversary of the unhappy armistice, a special votive lamp was set at the feet of the statue of Our Lady and kept burning day and night — a tradition going back to the Middle Ages.

Life in Paris was subdued. The German grip on the city was strong. Arrests and summary executions were frequent. But beneath the gray surface of submission,

131

The liberation of Paris from the Nazis was celebrated in a solemn ceremony at Notre-Dame on August 26, 1944. At right the hero of the day, Charles de Gaulle, greets General Leclerc, commander of the Second French Armored Division, in front of the cathedral.

of universal shortages and widespread fear, a spirit of opposition was gathering. An underground network developed, organized along tight conspiratorial lines. Activists carried out a campaign of harassment. Production was sabotaged. German patrols were ambushed, German soldiers shot under cover of darkness. Intelligence was gathered and transmitted, downed airmen and commandos sheltered, underground leaflets and newspapers distributed. The V for Victory sign, painted on walls, or two fingers surreptitiously lifted, kept alive the knowledge that a Resistance existed, and this knowledge strengthened the will to resist.

Young men faced with conscription into German labor brigades disappeared in the night. They went to the south and joined guerrilla bands operating in the rough terrain known as the *maquis*. Soon the name was being applied to the Resistance forces themselves. Armed with stolen weapons and with matériel dropped by British planes, they trained for the eventual rising. Others managed to get to England, crossing the Channel in small boats or taking the arduous route over the Pyrenees and escaping through Spain and Portugal. In England they joined the Free French forces headed by General Charles de Gaulle.

Until the general assumed this role, he had been a little-known figure. He had behind him the fairly standard career of a professional officer — service in World War I, a spell of teaching military history at Saint-Cyr, a post in the War Office, assignments in French Africa, command of an armored division on the Belgian front in 1940. He also had to his credit a remarkable but little-heeded book entitled *The Army of the Future*. De Gaulle had been named Undersecretary

of Defense in an ephemeral cabinet put together a few days after the surrender. When this fell, to be replaced by the more compliant government under the aged Marshal Pétain, de Gaulle went to England and lost no time announcing the existence of the Free French forces.

He had no easy time of it in England. The British and Americans were not disposed to take him as seriously as he expected. Concerned exclusively with military victory, they also had no sympathy for the political considerations with which de Gaulle seemed unnecessarily preoccupied. But he tenaciously upheld his claims and wrested support for his forces. Contingents of the Free French helped rout Rommel's army in the desert war and landed with the Allies in Italy. When the moment came for the full-scale invasion, de Gaulle was determined that the Free French should have a conspicuous role in the liberation of Paris.

Although few knew it, the city was in terrible jeopardy. The Germans had already been given orders for its destruction — orders that came directly from Hitler's headquarters. A special squad had been sent to Paris to prepare all the bridges for demolition. A master plan was drawn up for wrecking factories and power plants. All communications were to be shattered, and for symbolic purposes the historic monuments would be blown up. There were enough explosives on hand for the work. Dynamite was placed at the Eiffel Tower, the Invalides, and the Chamber of Deputies. Three tons of TNT were placed in the crypt of Notre-Dame.

Near the cathedral is the massive Prefecture of Police, and so the area around Notre-Dame became the very center of the crisis on August 19, 1944. After the Allied landing in Normandy, the Germans had taken the precaution of disarming the police. Now, with other civic employees, the entire Paris police force went on strike. A secret nest of Resistance fighters, the police responded to the first call for the uprising and seized their own headquarters. Almost at once, the long-planned insurrection broke out all over the city. Barricades were thrown up and street fighting began. Besieged inside the Prefecture, the Resistance forces hurled Molotov cocktails at the German tanks closing in on the building.

Meanwhile, couriers slipped through the German lines to reach the Allied armies, still a hundred miles away, and implore them to speed to Paris. Their strategy had called for bypassing Paris altogether in their eastward drive. But plans were revised, at least to the extent of sending the Second French Armored Division toward the capital. These troops made slow progress and took heavy losses, for the German defenses were still formidable. Once inside the city, there was more fighting to be done — clumsy, murderous combat between tanks and unexpected death from snipers' bullets. But on the night of August 24 the *bourdon* of Notre-Dame, mute for four years, gave the signal for a general tolling of the bells of Paris. The ringing of the church bells convinced the Germans that their cause was lost.

There was to be a Te Deum in the cathedral on August 26, 1944 — the first day the city was truly in French hands. General de Gaulle, on foot, his scanty forces following informally behind him, led a victory parade from the Arc de Triomphe to Notre-Dame. In thus exposing himself to enormous risk, either from enemy air attack, from German snipers, or from his

political foes, the general demonstrated again that indifference to consequences that was to become his special mark.

As he was about to enter Notre-Dame, rifle fire broke out, at first somewhere on the parvis, then inside the cathedral itself. The congregation, reflexes sharpened by four years' experience with war, hugged the floor. But de Gaulle moved imperturbably down the aisle to his seat in the transept. His example recalled others to a sense of proper bearing, and the ceremony began. Outside, the French forces were firing at the rooftops around the cathedral, against the presumptive snipers. A few suspects were taken into custody, but the mystery of who had done the firing was never solved.

After official peace, there were many political battles whose ultimate effect was to paralyze the state. Indochina flung off French rule, and the African territorial possessions, which had shown moving loyalty to France during the war, now asked for their reward in the form of independence. The most painful struggle took place in Algeria, legally a Department of France, with a sizable French population. There the French army obstinately took its final stand, under the slogan of *Algérie française* to counter the slogan of *Algérie libre*. The war there was particularly ugly, marked by terrorism and torture. It spread to France, especially to Paris, where bombings and assassinations became commonplace. There seemed no way out of the impasse. In 1958 Charles de Gaulle, who had withdrawn from public life, made his return. But to universal astonishment, de Gaulle, who seemed to have taken power to execute the will of the army, liquidated the war and let

Algeria go her own way. Only then was the country able to begin the immense tasks of reconstruction and modernization that had so long been delayed.

Charles de Gaulle headed the government for a decade, under a new constitution that greatly increased the power of the executive. Like Napoleon and Louis Napoleon, he made effective use of the plebiscite. Direct elections gave him overwhelming endorsement. He was sometimes likened, in his manners and policy, to a king. But he did not manifest the monarchical passion for palatial building. Instead, he fostered a program of public housing and highway construction and undertook as well the dramatic cleansing of the buildings of Paris.

Dictatorial but never a dictator, de Gaulle stepped down when the French people repudiated him in the elections of 1969. A year later, he died. In deliberate rejection of any conception of himself as a sovereign, Charles de Gaulle had left directions that his funeral was to be one of extreme simplicity. It took place at Colombey-Les-Deux-Eglises, the village in the Marne countryside where the de Gaulles had made their home since the 1930's. But the nation could not let the occasion go by without paying honor to the general. However much hostility had gathered around him in his years as president, no one could deny his stature. In proof of the worldwide respect he had earned, leaders from more than eighty nations came at short notice to attend the high requiem mass inside Notre-Dame.

Only a limited number of the general public had been admitted into the cathedral, but the public address system relayed the proceedings to the parvis. There some 70,000 persons waited, observing silence as had been requested. This being Anno Domini 1970, many had come with their transistor radios and could hear every word of the liturgy. Maurice de Sully, who eight hundred years earlier had conceived the cathedral on a grand scale so that it could accommodate the multitudes, would have found this perfectly in order.

After the ceremony, many of those who remembered de Gaulle as the hero of the Liberation made their way around to the rear of the cathedral. There, behind the apse, recent history meets ancient tradition. At the very end of the Île de la Cité, the waters of the Seine lapping against its walls, is the Monument to the Deportation. Dedicated to the 200,000 Frenchmen who died in German concentration camps, the monument is a crypt of concrete, like a wartime bunker, bomb shelter, or prison. Barred corridors heighten the impression of a prison house. Scratched on the walls, like the messages of the condemned in cells, are quotations from contemporary writers — Camus, Sartre, and other voices of the war years. This memorial to the martyred of World War II stands, like Notre-Dame herself, upon ground hallowed for many centuries. For here, in medieval times, was the priory of Saint-Denis-du-Pas, erected on the very spot where, according to legend, Saint Denis had been tortured before his execution.

Among the inscriptions on the wall of the crypt is one urging the modern pilgrim: "Forgive but do not forget."

Adorning the flèche of Notre-Dame is this statue of Saint Thomas with the facial features of Viollet-le-Duc.

NOTRE-DAME IN LITERATURE

Outraged and appalled by the dilapidated condition of the famed cathedral of Paris in the mid-nineteenth century, France's intellectual elite galvanized public opinion in support of restoration. A committee was formed, petitions were circulated, funds were solicited, and a competition for the best plan was held. Eugène Emmanuel Viollet-le-Duc, a leading architect and a fervent advocate of the contemporary Gothic revival, was awarded the commission. He began work in 1845 but the extensive restorations were not completed until 1864. In his Discourses on Architecture, *first published in 1860, Viollet-le-Duc praised the innovative twelfth-century architects who conceived and built the magnificent façade of Notre-Dame de Paris.*

Every one knows the front of Notre Dame de Paris; few perhaps realise the amount of knowledge, taste, study, care, resolution, and experience implied by the erection of that colossal pile within the space of at most ten or twelve years. Still it is an unfinished work; the two towers were to have been terminated by spires in stone, which would have completed and rendered intelligible the admirably designed lower masses. Here we have indeed Art, and Art of the noblest order. . . .

. . . First observe — what is of rare occurrence in buildings, particularly when they attain very considerable dimensions — that the architect has managed to divide his front by grand horizontal lines, which, without cutting it up into sections, form so many resting-places for the eye; that these divisions are made by an accomplished artist, inasmuch as they present spaces that are unequal, sometimes plain, sometimes ornamented, varied in their details, and yet presenting perfect unity in the entire effect. We have not here, as is so frequently to be seen in Roman, Byzantine, or modern buildings, the piling up of features that seem introduced at hap-hazard, and that might be changed, modified, or omitted. . . .

Above [the] basement, which, despite the profusion of sculpture spread beneath the arches, preserves an aspect of gravity and strength, there extends across the whole breadth of the front a gallery — a portico composed of hollowed lintels, supported on monolithic shafts surmounted by large capitals; in each opening is placed a colossal statue of a king. The architect, without interrupting his portico, took care to render apparent the projection of the buttresses; this cincture, which is of great severity in design and execution, and is low in proportion to the height of the front, has the effect of its actual dimensions restored by being surmounted by a balustrade which recalls the size of the human figure. Above, the buttresses continue upwards with offsets; but the three divisions of the front are set back to a considerable depth to leave a broad terrace over the Gallery of the Kings and to aid in giving this gallery great importance as a decorative line. . . .

. . . if from the examination of the general features we proceed to the details of the building, every one who understands construction will be amazed when he sees what numberless precautions are resorted to in the execution, — how the prudence of the practical builder is combined with the daring of the artist full of power and inventive imagination; while in examining the mouldings and the sculpture we remark the use of reliable methods, a scrupulous adherence to principles, a perfect appreciation of effect, a style unequalled in purity by modern art, an execution at the same time delicate and bold, quite free from exaggeration, and owing its merit to the study and love of form. . . .

The front of Notre Dame also renders conspicuous an excellence belonging exclusively to French architects at the time when France possessed an architecture of its own; that of variety in unity. At first sight the portals appear symmetrical; nevertheless the love of variety is evident; thus the doorway on the left is unlike that on the right. The north tower (that of the left) is sensibly larger than the south. On that side the arcading of the great gallery is more severe and solid than that of the other; whence we may conclude that — according to a custom generally followed — the two stone pieces would present dissimilarities in the details, though designed to present two equiponderant masses. We know how imperatively variety is required by our western genius. It is evident here as in other edifices built up at once in the same period, that the architect could not resolve to produce the same detail twice: in erecting two towers he gave a different drawing for each; and the increase of work he thereby imposed on himself was of no account with him in comparison with the *ennui* he would have experienced in letting his workmen execute two colossal towers exactly alike. Many find fault with these dissimilarities that contravene absolute symmetry; but it cannot be denied that in this craving for variety there is manifested an intellectual effort — a constant seeking for the better, — an emulation, shall I say, which is in accordance with our Western character.

EUGÈNE EMMANUEL VIOLLET-LE-DUC
Discourses on Architecture, 1860

In 1902 Hilaire Belloc — essayist, poet, historian, biographer, and novelist — wrote his famous panegyric to medieval Paris. The British author's devotion to Notre-Dame de Paris is matched only by his ire over the damage the cathedral suffered during the eighteenth century.

Notre Dame was built for a little Gothic capital, and a huge metropolis has outgrown her. The town was once, so to speak, the fringe of her garment; now she is but the centre of a circle miles around. . . . To a man who loves and knows the city, there soon comes a desire to communicate constantly with the memories of the Cathedral. And this desire, if he is wise, grows into a habit of coming close against the towers at evening, or of waiting under the great height of the nave for the voices of the Middle Ages.

Notre Dame thus lost in distance, central and remote, is like a lady grown old in a great house, about whose age new phrases and strange habits have arisen, who is surrounded with the youth of her own lineage, and yet is content to hear and understand without replying to their speech. She is silent in the midst of energy, and forgotten in the many activities of the household, yet she is the centre of the estate. . . .

The building of Notre Dame may be taken as a centre round which to group every characteristic of [the twelfth-century] renascence, which I have called a revolution. I have already insisted on the novelty of the Gothic spirit; I would now insist upon its daring. There was in all Paris nothing larger than buildings of from fifty to sixty yards in length, from thirty to forty feet in height. The Palace occupied a great area, but it was rather a group of buildings than one. Square towers here and there marked the churches; they were . . . of little height. But a man coming in from the countrysides would have seen, when Notre Dame was building, something typical on the

A drawing by Viollet-le-Duc of a gargoyle-adorned buttress from one of Notre-Dame's two towers

material side of what the mind of the twelfth century had been. For the first time in centuries upon centuries that creative passion for vastness, whose exaggeration is the enormous, but whose absence is the sure mark of pettiness and decline, had found expression. High above the broken line of the little flat grey town, one could see a great phalanx of scaffolding, up and thick like the spears of a company, and filled in with a mist of building and the distant noise of workmen. . . . Three times, four times the height of the tall things of the town, occupying in its bulk a notable division of the whole island, it would have made such a man think that for the future Paris would not hold a cathedral, but rather that the cathedral would make little Paris its neighbourhood. . . .

It was natural that the eighteenth century should have seen little in the Gothic glories of the thirteenth. There lay between the opening of our period and the last of the Gothic two hundred years . . . and these two hundred years were completely ignorant of the spirit which had built Notre Dame. The first of these centuries had indeed retained the old gables and deep lanes of medieval Paris . . . but the second . . . rebuilt Paris so completely that it destroyed even the outward example of a thing whose idea had long disappeared. Therefore the reign of Louis XIV had treated the Cathedral carelessly; had put in, just before the king's death, that huge, ugly high altar, and had destroyed the revered flooring of tombs to make way for the chess-board pattern of black and white that still displeases us. But throughout its action it left the shell and mass of Notre Dame the same. With the reign of Louis XV a very much worse spirit came upon the architects, for they were no longer content to neglect the old work, they were bent upon improving it. . . .

In the first place, they destroyed the old windows. It is written somewhere that the destruction began with the desire to let a shaft of white light come down upon the new high altar; even this insufficient excuse will hardly hold, for all the glass seems to have been taken away bodily and at one time, in 1741. We lost in that act the fulness and the spirit of Notre Dame, and the loss can never be made good. . . .

[Another] example of the evil done to Notre Dame was the action of Soufflot. I do not mean that heavy, great sacristy that he built, and that many men can still remember; I mean his curious restoration of the central door. Here was the chief glory of the West front. . . . Its carvings . . . were designed to symbolize the kernel of Christianity, and to make, as it were, a continual Credo for the people who passed beneath. . . . This door especially laid stress upon the end of man (which it showed in the Last Judgment carefully carved on the tympanum), and it had, on either side of the doorway, the twelve apostles listening to the teaching of Our Lord, whose statue stood in the central pier. . . . So, if the door was to have any meaning at all, the statue of Our Lord was its natural centre, the apostles whom He was teaching made the bulk of the design; and then, as a result and pendant to this, came the ogival tympanum above, with that subject of the Last Judgment which is the favourite theme of medieval Paris. The canopy carried over the Sacrament during processions was, in the Middle Ages in France (and is still in most countries), a flexible cloth, with four poles to support it. This, when a procession passed through a door, could be partly folded together if it was too wide to go through at its full stretch. Now it so happened that the canopy in the Church of France had been, of late times, made with a stiff framework;

Three sketches by Auguste Rodin of French ecclesiastical architecture

there was therefore a certain inconvenience and difficulty in passing through the main door on feast days, because the central pier divided it into two narrow portions. With this little pretext, the canons did not hesitate to ruin the principal door of their church. . . .

Since the main object was to widen the door, [Soufflot's] first act was to throw down the central pier, and to destroy the teaching Christ, for which, we may say, the whole porch existed. But even with this he was not content; for, looking at the heavy, triangular tympanum overhanging this broadened space, he thought to himself that it looked top-heavy, and might even fall, now that it lacked its old support. He therefore, very quietly and without comment, cut through the relief and the carving, brought his chisel just where a fine sweeping curve might be traced, dividing kings in the middle, cutting saints slantwise and removing angels, till he had opened a small ogive of his own within the greater one. Then he finished off the whole with a neat moulding. . . .

This hideous thing remained throughout the first part of our century, till Montalembert, in a fine speech, opened the reform, and saw the restoration of the Cathedral begun; and though, in that restoration, most of what was done was in reparation of what the Revolution destroyed, yet it is well to remember that the energy and the great schemes of the generation to which Montalembert and Viollet le Duc belonged were due to the Revolutionary movement, and that the sack and ruin of 1793 had been long prepared by the apathy and ignorance and forgetfulness of the generation preceding it. If Soufflot and the canons could see no beauty in, and could destroy the statuary of Notre Dame, it is not wonderful that the populace should deliberately throw down the memorials of a spirit of which they knew nothing, save that its heirs were then fighting the nation.

HILAIRE BELLOC
Paris, 1902

In the early years of the twentieth century Auguste Rodin, France's preeminent modern sculptor, was inspired by his periodic visits to the cathedrals scattered across the countryside. His profoundly personal notes, published in 1914 constitute a great artist's unique testament to the glory of French Gothic architecture, "the marvel of our marvels."

No one defends our Cathedrals.

The burden of old age crushes them, and under the pretext of curing them, of "restoring" what he should only uphold, the architect changes their features.

Crowds stop in silence before the Cathedrals, incapable of understanding the splendor of these architectural immensities, yet instinctively admiring them. Oh, the mute admiration of these crowds! I want to cry out to them that they are not mistaken; yes, our French Cathedrals are very beautiful! But their beauty is not easy to understand. Let us study them together; understanding will come to you as it has come to me. . . .

They still possess, despite all things and all persons, so much beauty, our old living stones! None has succeeded in killing them, and it is our duty to gather together and defend these relics.

Before I myself disappear, I wish at least to have told my admiration for them. I wish to pay them a debt of gratitude, I, who owe them so much happiness! I wish to honor these stones, so lovingly transformed into masterpieces by humble and wise artisans; these moldings admirably molded like the lips of a young woman; these beautiful lingering shadows where softness sleeps at the heart of power; these delicate and vigorous ribs springing up toward the vault and bending down upon the intersection of a flower; these rose windows whose magnificence was inspired by the setting sun or by the dawn. . . .

The art of the Middle Ages, in its ornamentation as well as in its constructions, derives from nature. It is therefore always to nature that one must go for an understanding of that art.

See Reims: in its tapestries we find the same color, leaves, and flowers as in its capitals. This is true of all the Cathedrals.

Then let us give ourselves the joy of studying these flowers in nature, that we may have a just notion of the resources which the decorator of living stones required of them. He penetrated the life of flowers by contemplating their forms, by analyzing their joys and their sorrows, their virtues and their weaknesses. These are our sorrows and our virtues.

So flowers have given the Cathedral.

To be convinced, go into the country and open your eyes.

At each step you will have a lesson in architecture. Men of yore looked before us and understood. They sought the plant in the stone and now we find their immortal stones in the eternal flowers. And (is this not the greatest homage they could have hoped for?) nature, although certainly without taking account of our dates, ceaselessly speaks to us of the 12th century, of the 15th, of the 14th, of the 18th. . . .

For me, these beautiful studies in the open air are beneficial. My room hurts me as shoes a size too small would hurt my feet. And how much more the city, the new city! It is in the fresh air of the fields and the woods, I must repeat, that I have learned all that I know.

As if thrown all at once into this immense garden in the beautiful sunshine, I feel myself live through my eyes a new, more intense, and unknown life. But so much splendor makes me dizzy. These flowers that a horticulturist grows for the seeds in massive squares filled with plants all alike, these juxtaposed layers of color, create an impression of stained glass and make me live with them.

It is too radiant. My powers are insufficient. I cannot endure the sudden burst of this beauty, of this motionless beauty! . . .

This eye of the anemone is angry and bloody. I know nothing more heart gripping than this flower. The one I am looking at is at the critical age; it is covered with fine wrinkles; its petals are as if disjointed; it is going to fall. The Persian vase in which I have placed it, blue, white, and cream, makes for it a worthy tomb. Its sisters in full bloom are designs for rose windows.

This large flower, of the violet color that I love in certain stained-glass windows of Notre Dame, touches me like a memory, especially now that we are returning to God, this flower and I. Its sad heart, where a black bud is forming, is also encircled by a black crown which the petals exaggerate, and these violet petals make the window seem to stand before the light. This flower is a widow.

AUGUSTE RODIN
Cathedrals of France, 1914

PROCESSIONS
AND PAGEANTS

Thomas Coryat, a "buffoon," or jester, at the court of King James I of England, embarked on a walking tour of the Continent in 1608. On one of his many stops he visited Notre-Dame de Paris. His quaint account of a feast day at the cathedral reveals both his Protestant distaste for sumptuous display and his grudging fascination with "Papist" extravagance.

About nine of the clock . . . in the morning, I went to the Cathedral Church which is dedicated to our Lady . . . to observe the strange ceremonies of [Corpus Christi] day, which for novelty sake, but not for any harty devotion . . . I was contented to behold, as being the first that ever I saw of that kinde, and I hartily wish they may be the last. No sooner did I enter into the Church but a great company of Clergy men came forth singing, and so continued all the time of the procession, till they returned unto the Church againe, some by couples, and some single. They walked partly in coapes [copes], whereof some were exceeding rich, being (in my estimation) worth at the least a hundred markes a peece; and partly in surplices. Also in the same traine there were many couples of little singing choristers, many of them not above eight or nine years old, and few above a dozen: which prety innocent punies were so egregiously deformed by those that had authority over them, that they could not choose but move great commiseration in any relenting spectator. For they had not a quarter so much haire left upon their heads as they brought with them into the world, out of their mothers wombs, being so clean shaved away round their whole heads that a man could perceive no more then the very rootes. A spectacle very pittifull (me thinks) to behold, though Papists esteeme it holy. The last man of the whole traine was the Bishop of Paris, a proper and comly man as any I saw in all the city, of some five and thirty years old. He walked not sub dio, that is under the open aire, as the rest did. But he had a rich cannopy carried over him, supported with many little pillers on both sides. This did the Priests carry: he himselfe was that day in his sumptuous Pontificalities, wearing religious ornaments of great price, like a second Aaron, with his Episcopall staffe in his hand, bending round at the toppe, called by us English men a Croisier, and his Miter on his head of cloth of silver, with two long labels hanging downe behind his neck. As for the streets of Paris they were more sumptuously adorned that day then any other day of the whole yeare, every street of speciall note being on both sides thereof, from the pentices of their houses to the lower end of the wall hanged with rich cloth of arras, and the costliest tapistry that they could provide. The shewes of our Lady street being so hyperbolical in pomp that day, that it exceeded the rest by many degrees. And for the greater addition of ornament to this feast of God, they garnished many of their streets with rich cupboords of plate as ever I saw in all my life. For they exposed upon their publique tables exceeding costly goblets, and what not tending to pompe, that is called by the name of plate. Upon the middest of their tables stood their golden Crucifixes, with divers other gorgeous Images. . . . Wherefore the foresaid sacred company, perambulating about some of the principall streets of Paris, especially our Lady street, were entertained with most divine honours. For whereas the Bishop carried the Sacrament, even his consecrated wafer cake, betwixt the Images of two golden Angels, whensoever he passed by any company, all the spectators prostrated themselves most humbly upon their knees, and elevated their handes with all possible reverence and religious behaviour, attributing as much divine adoration to the little wafer

The bishop leads a procession in honor of the reliquaries of Geneviève, patron saint of Paris.

cake, which they call the Sacrament of the Altar, as they could doe to Jesus Christ himselfe, if he were bodily present with them. If any Godly Protestant that hateth this superstition, should happen to be amongst them when they kneele, and forbeare to worship the Sacrament as they doe, perhaps he may be presently stabbed or otherwise most shamefully abused, if there should be notice taken of him. After they had spent almost two houres in these pompous (I will not say theatricall) shewes, they returned again to our Lady Church, where was performed very long and tedious devotion, for the space of two houres, with much excellent singing, and two or three solemne Masses, acted by the Bishops owne person.

THOMAS CORYAT
Coryat's Crudities, 1611

In 1793 the Committee of Public Safety abolished the worship of God in France. Nine years later the first consul, Napoleon Bonaparte, presided over the re-establishment of the Roman Catholic faith. J. G. Lemaistre, one of the first Englishmen to arrive in Paris following the temporary termination of hostilities between Great Britain and France, was an eyewitness to that historic ceremony, held at Notre-Dame on Easter Sunday 1802.

To day will probably be long remembered in the annals of France, on account of the promulgation of the law for the reestablishment of religion; on account of the definitive treaty of peace with England, the ratifications of which were exchanged this morning at the Thuilleries; and of the "Te Deum" sung at *Notre Dame,* in honour of these united events.

I wished very much to be present at a ceremony, which was rendered so particularly interesting by the number of curious concurring circumstances, too obvious to be detailed. Having no ticket, I went to the church at six o'clock in the morning, hoping to make my way, among the crowd, into those places, which were not appropriated to the constituted authorities. The doors were not open; and about a hundred persons, who were already arrived, stood enclosed in a kind of barrier, which seemed to have been put up for the purpose of preventing too great a press at the first opening of the gates. I placed myself against this bar, and hoped to gain admittance in the second division. I was soon followed and surrounded by a considerable crowd; and, after we had all remained about two hours in this uncomfortable state, a detachment of soldiers arrived, and attempted instantly to clear a passage. We were already so squeezed together, that it was impossible to make room for the military, without either losing our places, or incurring the danger of suffocation. When the soldiers perceived that, notwithstanding the blows which they dealt around them without ceremony, the people did not immediately make way, they lost all patience; and, not content with fixing their bayonets, called out for a detachment of horse. The brandishing of the one, and the fear of the other, soon dispersed the mob; but not till some had been wounded, and several severely bruised.

I could not help reflecting, with some degree of indignation, on this singular scene. In England, under a monarchical form of government, the military are not allowed to interfere, but in cases of positive danger, or actual insurrection; and even then under the orders of a civil magistrate. In France, where the system is called "republican," and every man is supposed to constitute a part of the sovereignty, the body of the people, coming quietly to see the first solemn service of that religion, which is said to be restored in compliance with their wishes, are driven with blows and military violence from the doors of that church, in which peace, liberty, equality, and good order, are about to be celebrated. . . .

It is needless for me to say, that I soon relinquished all hope of getting into the church, and thought myself happy in being able to make my escape unhurt from the claws of these heroes.

In going away, I perceived at the window of an adjoining hospital, nearly opposite the church, some ladies of my acquaintance, who were so obliging as to offer me a place near them, from which I might see the procession.

I had scarcely taken this situation, when a ticket for one of the privileged places in the church was given me by a person, who was unwilling to risk the difficulties, with which the approach to the doors seemed attended. After being sent about to different gates, I at last found admittance at one. When I reached the gallery, it was so completely full, that I found myself compelled to take refuge in the orchestra. From this situation I was again driven by the soldiers; and in despair I returned to the gallery, where, standing on the back of a tottering chair, and with at least twenty rows of spectators before me, I caught, not without some danger, a very imperfect glimpse of this splendid ceremony. . . .

The procession began with a numerous escort of different regiments. Among these were particularly remarked "les guides," a corps of handsome young men, clad in hussar dresses, and mounted on beautiful horses, who excited universal admiration. Next to them came the *"gens d'armes,"* or *"regiment d'élites,"* lately raised. They are men of a very respectable appearance, in blue uniforms, faced with yellow, whence long epaulets are suspended. These, as well as the buttons, are of silver, as is the lace of their hats. Their horses are black. The consular guards, and several regiments of the line, completed the military cavalcade. The ministers of state, and the "corps diplomatique," came next, and formed a long line of carriages. . . . A small corps of *Mamalukes* in their egyptian *costume,* some of whom led unmounted arabians, and a few aides-de-camp, immediately preceded the carriage, in which sat Bonaparte, accompanied by the other two consuls. His coach, new on the occasion, was simply elegant, and drawn by eight very fine horses richly caparisoned. His servants appeared in green coats and red waistcoats, on all the seams of which were rows of broad gold lace. The consuls were received at the door of the church by the archbishop of Paris, who placed over their head a *dais* (or canopy).

Bonaparte, with [the other consuls] *Cambaceres* on his right, and *le Brun* on his left hand, was conducted in this manner to a throne erected near the altar, under which their three chairs were placed. A similar throne appeared opposite, in which sat the cardinal legate.

The bishops bowed first to the altar, secondly to the consuls, and lastly to the cardinal. This was remarked by the public; as, under the monarchy, the representative of the pope was permitted to receive this homage before the sovereign of the country.

The oath settled by the *concordat* having been taken by the clergy, high mass was instantly said.

At the conclusion of this ceremony, M. *de Boisgelin,* formerly archbishop of Aix, lately named archbishop of Thoulouse, ascended the pulpit and

Parisians honor Sainte Geneviève.

delivered a discourse appropriate to the occasion. I regretted much, that the distance at which I was placed was so great, that it was impossible for me to hear the venerable preacher, who excited no little curiosity, from the singularity of his situation. He is the same man, who, at the *"sacre,"* or coronation, of Lewis XVI, preached in the same pulpit, before that unfortunate monarch. . . .

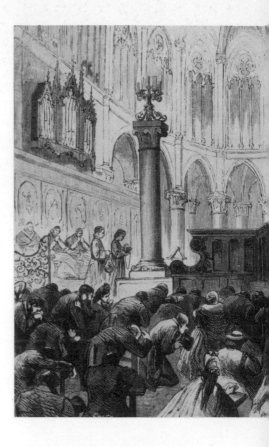

It was the custom formerly on these occasions, for the bishop, in beginning his discourse, to address himself to the king. A similar form was observed to day, and the expression of *"sire"* was exchanged for that of *"citoyen premier consul."* After the sermon, "Te Deum" was chanted. All the band of the opera house was employed, and *Lais* and *madame Bolla* supplied the vocal parts. The effect was fine, yet, comparatively, very inferiour to our musical meetings in Westminster abbey. . . .

The church was immensely full. The aisle was filled with the military, the different uniforms of which had a splendid effect. Behind the consuls sat the ambassadors, the ministers, and the generals. In a box above, at the entrance of the chapel, was placed madame Bonaparte, accompanied by her daughter and some other ladies. On the other side was a similar box, appropriate to the use of the ladies of the "corps diplomatique."

The two galleries or choirs, which surround the church, were divided into an orchestra for the music, seats for the different constituted authorities, and places for such individuals as were favoured with tickets. In the latter were of course seen all the persons at Paris most distinguished for situation, talent, or beauty. . . . The procession returned with the same ceremony as that in which it arrived; and all the streets of Paris were lined with spectators.

A discharge of sixty cannon was heard at the departure of the first consul from the Thuilleries; and his arrival at the church, and his return to the palace, were announced in the same manner. . . .

. . . Bonaparte was much applauded by the populace, in going to *Notre Dame*; and . . . *madame* received the same compliment, though she went there without any parade, in a plain handsome carriage, and seemed to decline, rather than to court, the notice of the public.

J. G. LEMAISTRE
A Rough Sketch of Modern Paris, 1802

SKEPTICAL REPORTS

Frances Trollope, the mother of Victorian novelist Anthony Trollope, established her reputation as a formidable social commentator with the publication in 1832 of Domestic Manners of the Americans, *a disparaging account of her three years' sojourn in Cincinnati, Ohio. In 1835 Mrs. Trollope studied the manners of the Parisians while attending a sermon given by the controversial Dominican monk Jean Baptiste Henri Lacordaire at Notre-Dame.*

The great reputation of [this] preacher induced us on Sunday to endure two hours more of tedious waiting before the mass which preceded the sermon began. It is only thus that a chair can be hoped for when the Abbé Lacordaire mounts the pulpit of Notre Dame. The penalty is really heavy; but having heard this celebrated person described as one who "appeared sent by Heaven to restore France to Christianity" — as "a hypocrite that set Tartuffe immeasurably in the background" — as "a man whose talent surpassed that of any preacher since Bossuet" — and as "a charlatan who ought to

harangue from a tub, instead of from the *chaire de Notre Dame de Paris*," —
I determined upon at least seeing and hearing him, however little I might
be able to decide on which of the two sides of the prodigious chasm that
yawned between his friends and enemies the truth was most likely to be
found. There were, however, several circumstances which lessened the te-
dium of this long interval: I might go farther, and confess that this period
was by no means the least profitable portion of the four hours which we
passed in the church.

On entering, we found the whole of the enormous nave railed in, as it
had been on Easter Sunday . . . upon applying at the entrance to this
enclosure, we were told that no ladies could be admitted to that part of the
church — but that the side aisles were fully furnished with chairs, and
afforded excellent places.

This arrangement astonished me in many ways: — first, as being so perfectly un-national; for go where you will in France, you find the best places
reserved for the women, — at least, this was the first instance in which I
ever found it otherwise. Next, it astonished me, because at every church I
had entered, the congregations, though always crowded, had been composed
of at least twelve women to one man. When, therefore, I looked over the
barrier upon the close-packed, well-adjusted rows of seats prepared to receive
fifteen hundred persons, I thought that unless all the priests in Paris came
in person to do honour to their eloquent confrère, it was very unlikely that
this uncivil arrangement should be found necessary. There was no time,
however, to waste in conjecture; the crowd already came rushing in at every
door, and we hastened to secure the best places that the side aisles afforded.
We obtained seats between the pillars immediately opposite to the pulpit,
and felt well enough contented, having little doubt that a voice which had
made itself heard so well must have power to reach even to the side aisles of
Notre Dame.

The first consolation which I found for my long waiting, after placing
myself in that attitude of little ease which the straight-backed chair allowed,
was from the recollection that the interval was to be passed within the venerable walls of Notre Dame. It is a glorious old church, and though not com-
parable in any way to Westminster Abbey, or to Antwerp, or Strasburg, or
Cologne, or indeed to many others which I might name, has enough to
occupy the eye very satisfactorily for a considerable time. The three elegant
rose-windows, throwing in their coloured light from north, west, and south,
are of themselves a very pretty study for half an hour or so; and besides, they
brought back, notwithstanding their miniature diameter of forty feet, the
remembrance of the magnificent circular western window of Strasburg —
the recollection of which was almost enough to while away another long
interval. . . .

I had another source of amusement, and by no means a trifling one, in
watching the influx of company. The whole building soon contained as many
human beings as could be crammed into it; and the seats, which we thought,
as we took them, were very so-so places indeed, became accommodations for
which to be most heartily thankful. Not a pillar but supported the backs of
as many men as could stand round it; and not a jutting ornament, the balustrade of a side altar, or any other "point of 'vantage," but looked as if a
swarm of bees were beginning to hang upon it.

But the sight which drew my attention most was that displayed by the

*The Archbishop of Paris blesses
the faithful in Notre-Dame.*

147

exclusive central aisle. When told that it was reserved for gentlemen, I imagined of course that I should see it filled by a collection of staid-looking, middle-aged, Catholic citizens, who were drawn together from all parts of the town, and perhaps the country too, for the purpose of hearing the celebrated preacher: but, to my great astonishment, instead of this I saw pouring in by dozens at a time, gay, gallant, smart-looking young men, such indeed as I had rarely seen in Paris on any other religious occasion. Amongst these was a sprinkling of older men; but the great majority were decidedly under thirty....

... the organ pealed, the fine chant of the voices was heard above it, and in a few minutes we saw the archbishop and his splendid train escorting the Host to its ark upon the altar.

During the interval between the conclusion of the mass and the arrival of the Abbé Lacordaire in the pulpit, my sceptical neighbour ... addressed me.

"Are you prepared to be very much enchanted by what you are going to hear?" said he.

"I hardly know what to expect," I replied....

"You will find that he has a prodigious flow of words, much vehement gesticulation, and a very impassioned manner. This is quite sufficient to establish his reputation for eloquence among *les jeunes gens*."

"But I presume you do not yourself subscribe to the sentence pronounced by these young critics?"

"Yes I do, — as far, at least, as to acknowledge that this man has not attained his reputation without having displayed great ability. But though all the talent of Paris has long consented to receive its crown of laurels from the hands of her young men, it would be hardly reasonable to expect that their judgment should be as profound as their power is great."

"Your obedience to this beardless synod is certainly very extraordinary," said I: "I cannot understand it."

"I suppose not," said he, laughing; "it is quite a Paris fashion; but we all seem contented that it should be so. If a new play appears, its fate must be decided by *les jeunes gens*; if a picture is exhibited, its rank amidst the works of modern art can only be settled by them: does a dancer, a singer, an actor, or a preacher appear — a new member in the tribune, or a new prince upon the throne, — it is still *les jeunes gens* who must pass judgment on them all; and this judgment is quoted with a degree of deference utterly inconceivable to a stranger."

... I glanced my eye towards the pulpit, but it was still empty; and on looking round me, I perceived that all eyes were turned in the direction of a small door in the north aisle, almost immediately behind us. "Il est entré là!" said a young woman near us, in a tone that seemed to indicate a feeling deeper than respect, and, in truth, not far removed from adoration. Her eyes were still earnestly fixed upon the door, and continued to be so, as well as those of many others, till it reopened and a slight young man in the dress of a priest prepared for the *chaire* [pulpit] appeared at it. A verger made way for him through the crowd, which, thick and closely wedged as it was, fell back on each side of him, as he proceeded to the pulpit, with much more docility than I ever saw produced by the clearing a passage through the intervention of a troop of horse.

Silence the most profound accompanied his progress; I never witnessed more striking demonstrations of respect: and yet it is said that three-fourths

The 1864 consecration of the newly restored Notre-Dame

of Paris believe this man to be a hypocrite. . . .

It is easier to describe to you everything which preceded the sermon, than the sermon itself. This was such a rush of words, such a burst and pouring out of passionate declamation, that even before I had heard enough to judge of the matter, I felt disposed to prejudge the preacher, and to suspect that his discourse would have more of the flourish and furbelow of human rhetoric than of the simplicity of divine truth in it.

His violent action, too, disgusted me exceedingly. The rapid and incessant movement of his hands, sometimes of one, sometimes of both, more resembled that of the wings of a humming-bird than anything else I can remember. . . .

. . . I cannot remember having ever heard a preacher I less liked, reverenced, and admired, than this new Parisian saint. . . .

In describing the two hours' prologue to the mass, I forgot to mention that many young men — not in the reserved places of the centre aisle, but sitting near us, beguiled the tedious interval by reading. Some of the volumes they held had the appearance of novels from a circulating library, and others were evidently collections of songs, probably less spiritual than *spirituels*.

The whole exhibition certainly showed me a new page in the history of *Paris as it is,* and I therefore do not regret the four hours it cost me: but once is enough.

FRANCES TROLLOPE
Paris and the Parisians in 1835, 1836

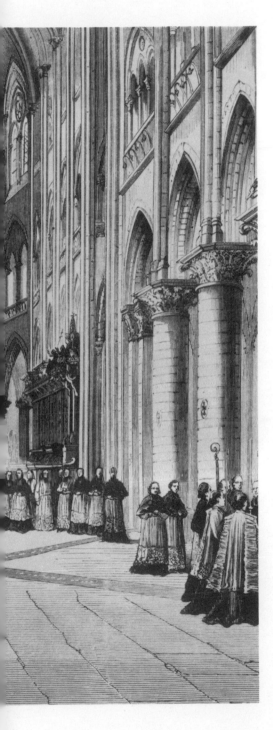

Samuel Langhorne Clemens — better known by his pen name, Mark Twain — gently spoofed the sentimental travel books of the nineteenth century in The Innocents Abroad, *based on a series of letters he wrote in 1869 as a roving European correspondent. While in France, America's foremost storyteller and humorist made an obligatory stop at Notre-Dame de Paris.*

We went to see the Cathedral of Notre Dame. We had heard of it before. It surprises me, sometimes, to think how much we *do* know, and how intelligent we are. We recognised the brown old Gothic pile in a moment; it was like the pictures. We stood at a little distance and changed from one point of observation to another, and gazed long at its lofty square towers and its rich front, clustered thick with stony, mutilated saints who had been looking calmly down from their perches for ages. The Patriarch of Jerusalem stood under them in the old days of chivalry and romance, and preached the third Crusade, more than six hundred years ago; and since that day they have stood there and looked quietly down upon the most thrilling scenes, the grandest pageants, the most extraordinary spectacles that have grieved or delighted Paris. These battered and broken-nosed old fellows saw many and many a cavalcade of mail-clad knights come marching home from the Holy Land; they heard the bells above them toll the signal for the St. Bartholomew's Massacre, and they saw the slaughter that followed; later, they saw the Reign of Terror, the carnage of the Revolution, the overthrow of a king, the coronation of two Napoleons, the christening of the young prince that lords it over a regiment of servants in the Tuileries to-day — and they may possibly continue to stand there until they see the Napoleon dynasty swept away and the banners of a great Republic floating above its ruins. I wish

these old parties could speak. They could tell a tale worth the listening to.

They say that a pagan temple stood where Notre Dame now stands, in the old Roman days, eighteen or twenty centuries ago — remains of it are still preserved in Paris; and that a Christian church took its place about A.D. 300; another took the place of that in A.D. 500; and that the foundations of the present Cathedral were laid about A.D. 1100. The ground ought to be measurably sacred by this time, one would think. One portion of this noble old edifice is suggestive of the quaint fashions of ancient times. It was built by Jean Sans-Peur, Duke of Burgundy, to set his conscience at rest — he had assassinated the Duke of Orleans. Alas! those good old times are gone, when a murderer could wipe the stain from his name and soothe his troubles to sleep simply by getting out his bricks and mortar and building an addition to a church. . . .

We loitered through the grand aisles for an hour or two, staring up at the rich stained glass windows embellished with blue and yellow and crimson saints and martyrs, and trying to admire the numberless great pictures in the chapels, and then we were admitted to the sacristy and shown the magnificent robes which the Pope wore when he crowned Napoleon I.; a waggon-load of solid gold and silver utensils used in the great public processions and ceremonies of the Church; some nails of the true cross, a fragment of the cross itself, a part of the crown of thorns. We had already seen a large piece of the true cross in a church in the Azores, but no nails. They showed us likewise the bloody robe which that Archbishop of Paris wore who exposed his sacred person and braved the wrath of the insurgents of 1848, to mount the barricades and hold aloft the olive branch of peace in the hope of stopping the slaughter. His noble effort cost him his life. He was shot dead. They showed us a cast of his face, taken after death, the bullet that killed him, and the two vertebrae in which it lodged. These people have a somewhat singular taste in the matter of relics. Ferguson told us that the silver cross which the good Archbishop wore at his girdle was seized and thrown into the Seine, where it lay embedded in the mud for fifteen years, and then an angel appeared to a priest and told him where to dive for it; he *did* dive for it and got it, and now it is there on exhibition at Notre Dame, to be inspected by anybody who feels an interest in inanimate objects of miraculous intervention.

SAMUEL LANGHORNE CLEMENS
The Innocents Abroad, 1869

AN INSPIRATION
FOR NATIVE SONS

The novel Gargantua — *a bawdy and boisterous satire of French written by the sixteenth-century humanist François Rabelais — recounts the extraordinary adventures of an amiable family of giants. In this excerpt from Book I, Gargantua steals the bells of Notre-Dame and meets a pedantic theologian.*

Gargantua considered the great bells in the Towers of Notre Dame and made them ring out most harmoniously. The music suggested to him that they might sound very sweet tinkling on his mare's neck when he sent her back to his father laden with Brie cheese and fresh herring. So he promptly picked up the bells of the Cathedral and carried them home. . . .

The whole city was in an uproar, for Parisians, as you know, are ever prone to insurrection. Indeed, foreigners marvel at the patience of French

Rabelais's gentle giant, Gargantua, towers over the cathedral of Paris.

kings who, faced with troubles arising daily out of the mob's violence, will not justifiedly stamp them out at their source. . . .

You will readily believe that the place where all these people stormed and rioted was the royal Hotel de Nesle, then the seat of the University Court, but now no longer the site of the Oracle of Lutetia. Here the whole grievance of the stolen bells was discussed and deplored. After extensive argumentation *pro* and *con*, they moved . . . to empower the oldest and most authoritative member of the faculty to apprize Gargantua of the dreadful damage they suffered through the loss of these bells. Despite certain objections that this mission could be better fulfilled by an orator than by a divine, our Master Janotus de Bragmardo, Doctor of Theology, was delegated.

Master Janotus, with a haircut like that affected by Julius Caesar, settled the traditional doctoral hood over his cootlike head. Next, he antidoted his stomach against possible contamination, with cakes baked in the most secular ovens, and holy water from his excellently stocked cellar. Then, he proceeded to Gargantua's. Before him crawled three black beadles; behind him he dragged five or six servile and artless Masters of Arts. . . .

. . . Gargantua, learning what had happened, called aside his tutor Ponocrates, his steward Philotomus — the name means a lover of carving — his esquire Gymnastes ("teacher of esthetics") and Eudemon. A summary conference was held instanter to plan their reply and subsequent actions. It was unanimously agreed to take the learned doctors to the conservatory or wine room and there make them drink uproariously. Thus this wheezing old dryasdust would be denied the vainglory of supposing the bells had been restored at his request, for, while he tippled, they would summon the Provost of the City, the Rector of the University and the Vicar-General to the Bishop of Paris. To these officers they would hand over the bells ere ever the old sophister had delivered his message. . . .

Which is exactly what happened. The authorities arrived, our theologian was ushered into the official meeting, and having hawked and spluttered, began as follows.

"Ahem, hem, hem! *B'na dies,* Sir, g'day to you, *b'nadies vobis* and g'day to you, gentlemen. It were but right that you should return our bells, for we are in sore need of them! Hem, ahem, ughsh! Many a time we have heretofore refused good money for them from the citizens of London (near Cahors) and of Bordeaux (in the land of Brie). These aspired to purchase our bells for the substantific quality of their elementary complexion which is intronificated in the terrestrality of their quidditative nature to extraneize the tempests and hurricanes that fall upon our vines. . . .

"If you restore them to us at my request, I shall gain one and one-quarter yards of sausage by it. And a fine pair of breeches, too, which will do my legs a lot of good — or, if I don't, then they'll have broken their promise! . . .

"O Sir, *Domine, restor bellsimus nobis,* give us back our bells! Truly, *est bonum urbis,* it is for the good of the city. Every one here uses them. If your mare enjoys them, so does our faculty. . . .

"*Omnis bella bellabilis, in bellerio bellando, bellans bellativo bellare bellantes. Parisius habet bellas. Ergo Gluc.* Every bellable bell, to be belled in the belfry, belling by the bellative, makes the bellers bell bellfully! In Paris there are bells. Q.E.D. . . ."

FRANÇOIS RABELAIS
Gargantua, 1535

Hugo's "hunchback of Notre-Dame" frightens a would-be assailant.

In his introduction to Notre-Dame de Paris, *Victor Hugo exhorted the reader: "Let us, if possible, inspire the nation with the love of national architecture. That, the author declares, is one of the principal objects of this book; that, one of the principal objects of his life." Hugo's epic novel is, of course, far more than a polemic: it is the poignant story of the tragic hunchback, Quasimodo.*

Now, in 1482, Quasimodo had grown up. He had been made, some years previous, bell-ringer of Notre-Dame, thanks to his adopted father, Claude Frollo. . . . In time, a peculiar bond of intimacy grew up between the ringer and the church. Cut off forever from the world by the double fatality of his unknown birth and his deformity, confined from infancy in this doubly insuperable circle, the poor wretch became used to seeing nothing of the world outside the religious walls which had received him into their shadow. Notre-Dame had been to him by turns, as he grew and developed, egg, nest, home, country, universe.

And it is certain that there was a sort of mysterious and pre-existing harmony between this creature and the structure. When, still a child, he dragged himself tortuously and jerkingly along beneath its gloomy arches, he seemed, with his human face and animal-like limbs, to be some reptile native to that damp dark pavement upon which the Roman capitals cast so many grotesque shadows.

Later on, the first time that he mechanically grasped the bell-rope in the tower, and clung to it, and set the bell ringing, he seemed to Claude, his adopted father, like a child whose tongue is loosed, and who begins to talk.

It was thus, little by little, growing ever after the pattern of the cathedral, living there, sleeping there, seldom leaving its precincts, forever subject to its mysterious influence, he came to look like it, to be imbedded in it, to form, as it were, an integral part of it. His sharp angles (if we may be pardoned the simile) fitted into the re-entering angles of the building, and he seemed not only to inhabit it, but to be its natural tenant. He might almost be said to have assumed its form, as the snail assumes the form of its shell. It was his dwelling, his hole, his wrapper. There was so deep an instinct of sympathy between him and the old church, there were so many magnetic affinities between them, that he in some sort clung to it, as the tortoise to its shell. The rugged cathedral was his shell. . . .

. . . This dwelling was his own. It contained no deeps which Quasimodo had not penetrated, no heights which he had not scaled. He often climbed the façade several stories high by the mere aid of projecting bits of sculpture. The towers upon the outer face of which he was frequently seen crawling like a lizard gliding over a perpendicular wall — those twin giants, so lofty, so threatening, so terrible — had no vertigoes, no terrors, no giddiness for him. They were so docile to his hand, so easily climbed, that he might be said to have tamed them. . . .

Moreover, not only his body but also his spirit seemed to be moulded by the cathedral. What was the state of that soul? What bent had it assumed, what form had it taken under its knotty covering in this wild life? It would be hard to tell. Quasimodo was born blind of one eye, humpbacked, lame. It was only by great patience and great painstaking that Claude Frollo had succeeded in teaching him to speak. But a fatality followed the poor foundling. Bell-ringer of Notre-Dame at the age of fourteen, a new infirmity soon put the finishing touch to his misfortunes; the bells had broken the drum of his ears: he became deaf. . . .

. . . he never turned his face to the world of men save with regret; his cathedral was enough for him. It was peopled with marble figures, kings, saints, and bishops who at least did not laugh at him, and never looked upon him otherwise than with peace and good-will. The other statues, those of monsters and demons, did not hate Quasimodo; he looked too much like them for that. They rather mocked at other men. The saints were his friends, and blessed him. The monsters were his friends, and protected him. . . .

And the cathedral was not only company for him, it was the universe; nay, more, it was Nature itself. He never dreamed that there were other hedge-rows than the stained-glass windows in perpetual bloom; other shade than that of the stone foliage always budding, loaded with birds in the thickets of Saxon capitals; other mountains than the colossal towers of the church; or other oceans than Paris roaring at their feet.

But that which he loved more than all else in the motherly building, that which awakened his soul and bade it spread its poor stunted wings folded in such misery where it dwelt in darkness, that which sometimes actually made him happy, was the bells. He loved them, he caressed them, he talked to them, he understood them. From the chime in the steeple over the transept to the big bell above the door, he had a tender feeling for them all. The belfry of the transept and the two towers were to him like three great cages, in which the birds, trained by him, sang for him alone; and yet it was these very bells which made him deaf. . . .

It is impossible to give any idea of his joy on those days when full peals were rung. When the archdeacon dismissed him with the word "Go," he ran up the winding staircase more rapidly than any one else could have gone down. He reached the aerial chamber of the big bell, breathless; he gazed at it an instant with love and devotion, then spoke to it gently, and patted it, as you would a good horse about to take a long journey. He condoled with it on the hard work before it. After these initiatory caresses he called to his assistants, stationed on a lower story of the tower, to begin. They then hung upon the ropes, the windlass creaked, and the enormous mass of metal moved slowly. Quasimodo, panting with excitement, followed it with his eye. The first stroke of the clapper upon its brazen wall made the beam on which he stood quiver. Quasimodo vibrated with the bell. "Here we go! There we go!" he shouted with a mad burst of laughter. But the motion of the great bell grew faster and faster, and as it traversed an ever-increasing space, his eye grew bigger and bigger, more and more glittering and phosphorescent. At last the full peal began; the whole tower shook: beams, leads, broad stones, all rumbled together, from the piles of the foundation to the trefoils at the top. Then Quasimodo's rapture knew no bounds: he came and went; he trembled and shook from head to foot with the tower. The bell, let loose, and frantic with liberty, turned its jaws of bronze to either wall of the tower in turn, — jaws from which issued that whirlwind whose roar men heard for four leagues around. Quasimodo placed himself before those gaping jaws; he rose and fell with the swaying of the bell, inhaled its tremendous breath, gazed now at the abyss swarming with people like ants, two hundred feet below him, and now at the huge copper clapper which from second to second bel-lowed in his ear. That was the only speech which he could hear, the only sound that broke the universal silence reigning around him. He basked in it as a bird in the sunshine. All at once the frenzy of the bell seized him; his

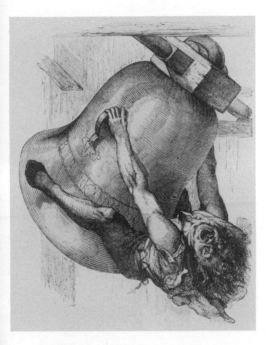

At left, a fanciful gargoyle observes the city; above, Quasimodo swings joyfully on Notre-Dame's huge bell.

look became strange; he waited for the passing of the bell as a spider lies in wait for a fly, and flung himself upon it. Then, suspended above the gulf, launched upon the tremendous vibration of the bell, he grasped the brazen monster by its ears, clasped it with his knees, spurred it with his heels, doubling the fury of the peal with the whole force and weight of his body. As the tower shook, he shouted and gnashed his teeth, his red hair stood erect, his chest labored like a blacksmith's bellows, his eye flashed fire, the monstrous steed neighed and panted under him; and then the big bell of Notre-Dame and Quasimodo ceased to exist: they became a dream, a whirlwind, a tempest; vertigo astride of uproar; a spirit clinging to a winged crupper; a strange centaur, half man, half bell. . . .

The presence of this extraordinary being pervaded the whole cathedral with a peculiar breath of life. It seemed, at least in the opinion of the grossly superstitious mob, as if mysterious emanations issued from him, animating every stone in Notre-Dame and making the very entrails of the old church throb and palpitate. His mere presence there was enough to lead the vulgar to fancy that the countless statues in the galleries and over the doors moved and breathed. And in very truth the cathedral seemed a creature docile and obedient to his hand: it awaited his pleasure to lift up its mighty voice; it was possessed and filled with Quasimodo as with a familiar spirit. He might be said to make the vast edifice breathe. He was indeed omnipresent in it, he multiplied himself at every point of the structure. Sometimes the terrified spectator saw an odd dwarf on the extreme pinnacle of one of the towers, climbing, creeping, writhing, crawling on all fours, descending head-first into the abyss, leaping from one projection to another, and diving deep into the maw of some sculptured gorgon: it was Quasimodo hunting for daws' nests. Sometimes a visitor stumbled over a sort of living nightmare, crouching and scowling in a dark corner of the church: it was Quasimodo absorbed in thought. Sometimes an enormous head and a bundle of ill-adjusted limbs might be seen swaying frantically to and fro from a rope's end under a belfry: it was Quasimodo ringing the Vespers of the Angelus. Often by night a hideous form was seen wandering along the frail delicately-wrought railing which crowns the towers and runs around the top of the chancel: it was still the hunchback of Notre-Dame. Then, so the neighbors said, the whole church took on a fantastic, supernatural, horrible air, — eyes and mouths opened wide here and there; the dogs and dragons and griffins of stone which watch day and night, with outstretched necks and gaping jaws, around the monstrous cathedral, barked loudly. And if it were a Christmas night, while the big bell, which seemed uttering its death-rattle, called the faithful to attend the solemn midnight mass, the gloomy façade assumed such an aspect that it seemed as if the great door were devouring the crowd while the rose-window looked on. And all this was due to Quasimodo. Egypt would have taken him for the god of the temple; the Middle Ages held him to be its demon: he was its soul.

So much so that to those who know that Quasimodo once existed, Notre-Dame is now deserted, inanimate, dead. They feel that something has gone from it. That immense body is empty; it is a skeleton; the spirit has left it, the abode remains, and that is all. It is like a skull; the sockets of the eyes are still there, but sight is gone.

VICTOR HUGO
Notre-Dame de Paris, 1831

*Based on the legend of the sinner condemned to wander aimlessly through eternity,
The Wandering Jew, written by the nineteenth-century French novelist Eugène
Sue, is a complex melodrama of greed, prejudice, and treachery. In this scene
the famed cathedral of Paris becomes the setting for a macabre masquerade.*

Of all the quarters of Paris that which, during the period of the increase of
the cholera, offered what was, perhaps, the most fearful spectacle, was the
Quartier de la Cité; and, in the Cité, the façade of Notre-Dame was almost
every day the theatre of terrible scenes, as the majority of the sick of the
neighboring streets, whom they were conveying to the Hôtel Dieu, were
brought to this spot.

The cholera had not one physiognomy — it had a thousand. Thus, . . .
several events in which the horrible mingled with the strange took place in
the front of Notre-Dame. . . .

On the black and cracked wall of the arcade might be read a placard
recently put up. . . .

*"Vengeance! vengeance! The people who are conveyed to the hospitals
are poisoned there, because they find the numbers of sick too many. Every
night boats filled with dead carcasses go down the Seine! Vengeance and
death to the murderers of the people! . . ."*

The sun was beginning to set, and threw his golden beams on the black
sculpture of the portal of Notre-Dame and the imposing mass of its two
towers, which rose in the midst of a perfectly blue sky. . . .

. . . there were heard the noisy sounds of joyous music, and repeated cries,
as it advanced, of *"The cholera masquerade!"*

These words bespoke one of those episodes, half buffoon, half terrible, yet
scarcely credible, which marked the progress of this scourge.

In truth, if contemporary testimony was not completely accordant with
the details of the public papers on the subject of this masquerade, we should
say, that instead of an actual fact, it was the invention of some demented
brain. *The masquerade of the cholera* came into the square of Notre-
Dame. . . .

The masquerade was composed of a four-wheeled car, escorted by men and
women on horseback; cavaliers and amazons wore fancy costumes. . . .

There had been a rumor that a masquerade had been organized with the
intention of *bullying* . . . the *Cholera,* and, by a merry display, raise the
spirits of the frightened populace; and thus artists, young men of fashion,
students, clerks, etc., had answered the appeal, and, although up to this
period unknown to each other, they *fraternized* immediately. Many of them,
to complete the fête, brought their lady-loves. A subscription had covered
the expenses of the fête, and on the morning, after a splendid breakfast at the
further end of Paris, the joyous group had started bravely on their way to
conclude the day by a dinner in the square of Notre-Dame.

We said *bravely,* because it required in the young females a singular
strength of mind, an unusual firmness of character, in order thus to traverse
this great city, plunged in consternation and amazement, to cross at every
turn litters charged with the dying, and vehicles loaded with the dead, in
order to attack, by the strangest pleasantry, the scourge that was decimating
Paris.

EUGÈNE SUE
The Wandering Jew, 1845

156

*Soufflot's mutilation of Notre-Dame's
central portal is visible in this
nineteenth-century engraving.*

"CATHEDRAL LIKE A ROCK"

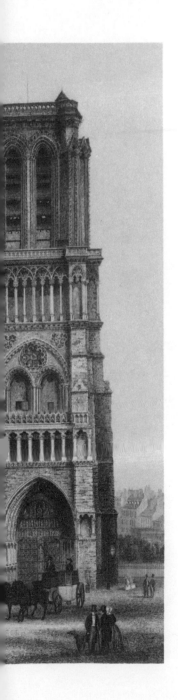

Henry James's 1903 novel The Ambassadors *portrays the moral dilemma of a middle-aged American in Paris. Torn between his mission as an "ambassador" — to rescue his fiancée's son from the clutches of Mme. de Vionnet, a sophisticated Frenchwoman — and his growing realization that life may be more meaningful in Europe, Lambert Strether seeks solace within Notre-Dame de Paris.*

It was not the first time Strether had sat alone in the great dim church — still less was it the first of his giving himself up, so far as conditions permitted, to its beneficent action on his nerves. He had been to Notre Dame with [several friends], and had found the place, even in company, such a refuge from the obsession of his problem that, with renewed pressure from that source, he had not unnaturally recurred to a remedy that seemed so, for the moment, to meet the case. He was conscious enough that it was only for the moment, but good moments — if he could call them good — still had their value for a man who, by this time, struck himself as living almost disgracefully from hand to mouth. Having so well learnt the way, he had lately made the pilgrimage more than once by himself — had quite stolen off, taking an unnoticed chance and making no point of speaking of the adventure when restored to his friends. . . .

. . . [The] impulse that had now carried him across to Notre Dame [was] the impulse to let things be, to give them time to justify themselves or at least to pass. He was aware of having no errand in such a place but the desire not to be, for the hour, in certain other places; a sense of safety, of simplification, which, each time he yielded to it, he amused himself by thinking of as a private concession to cowardice. The great church had no altar for his worship, no direct voice for his soul; but it was none the less soothing even to sanctity; for he could feel while there what he couldn't elsewhere, that he was a plain tired man taking the holiday he had earned. He was tired, but he wasn't plain — that was the pity and the trouble of it; he was able, however, to drop his problem at the door very much as if it had been the copper piece that he deposited, on the threshold, in the receptacle of the inveterate blind beggar. He trod the long, dim nave, sat in the splendid choir, paused before the clustered chapels of the east end, and the mighty monument laid upon him its spell. He might have been a student under the charm of a museum — which was exactly what, in a foreign town, in the afternoon of life, he would have liked to be free to be. . . .

. . . He had the habit, in these contemplations, of watching a fellow-visitant, here and there, from a respectable distance, remarking some note of behavior, of penitence, of prostration, of the absolved, relieved state; this was the manner in which his vague tenderness took its course, the degree of demonstration to which, naturally, it had to confine itself. It had not indeed so felt its responsibility as when, on this occasion, he suddenly measured the suggestive effect of a lady whose supreme stillness, in the shade of one of the chapels, he had two or three times noticed as he made, and made once more, his slow circuit. She was not prostrate — not in any degree bowed, but she was strangely fixed, and her prolonged immobility showed her, while he passed and paused, as wholly given up to the need, whatever it was, that had brought her there. She only sat and gazed before her, as he himself often sat; but she had placed herself, as he never did, within the focus of the shrine, and she had lost herself, he could easily see, as he would only have liked to do. She was not a wandering alien, keeping back more than she gave, but one

157

of the familiar, the intimate, the fortunate, for whom these dealings had a method and a meaning. She reminded our friend — since it was the way of nine-tenths of his current impressions to act as recalls of things imagined — of some fine, firm, concentrated heroine of an old story, something he had heard, read, something that, had he had a hand for drama, he might himself have written, renewing her courage, renewing her clearness, in splendidly-protected meditation. Her back, as she sat, was turned to him, but his impression absolutely required that she should be young and interesting, and she carried her head, moreover, even in the sacred shade, with a discernible faith in herself, a kind of implied conviction of consistency, security, impunity. But what had such a woman come for if she hadn't come to pray? Strether's reading of such matters was, it must be owned, confused; but he wondered if her attitude were some congruous fruit of absolution, of "indulgence." He knew but dimly what indulgence, in such a place, might mean; yet he had, as with a soft sweep, a vision of how it might indeed add to the zest of active rites. All this was a good deal to have been denoted by a mere lurking figure who was nothing to him; but, the last thing before leaving the church, he had the surprise of a still deeper quickening.

He had dropped upon a seat half-way down the nave and, again in the museum mood, was trying with head thrown back and eyes aloft, to reconstitute a past, to reduce it in fact to the convenient terms of Victor Hugo, whom, a few days before, giving the rein for once in a way to the joy of life, he had purchased in seventy bound volumes, a miracle of cheapness, parted with, he was assured by the shopman, at the price of the red-and-gold alone. . . . Turning, he saw that a lady stood there as for a greeting, and he sprang up as he next perceived that the lady was Mme. de Vionnet, who appeared to have recognized him as she passed near him on her way to the door. She checked, quickly and gayly, a certain confusion in him, came to meet it, turned it back, by an art of her own; the confusion threatened him as he knew her for the person he had lately been observing. She was the lurking figure of the dim chapel; she had occupied him more than she guessed; but it came to him in time, luckily, that he needn't tell her and that no harm, after all, had been done. She herself, for that matter, straightway showed that she felt their encounter as the happiest of accidents — had for him a "You come here too?" that despoiled surprise of every awkwardness.

"I come often," she said; "I love this place; but I'm terrible, in general, for churches. The old women who live in them all know me; in fact I'm already myself one of the old women. It's like that, at all events, that I foresee I shall end." Looking about for a chair, so that he instantly pulled one nearer, she sat down with him again to the sound of an "Oh, I like so much your also being fond — !"

He confessed the extent of his feeling, though she left the object vague; and he was struck with the tact, the taste of her vagueness, which simply took for granted in him a sense of beautiful things. . . .

. . . They talked, in low, easy tones and with lifted, lingering looks, about the great monument and its history and its beauty — all of which, Mme. de Vionnet professed, came to her most in the other, the outer view. "We'll presently, after we go," she said, "walk round it again if you like. I'm not in a particular hurry, and it will be pleasant to look at it again with you."

HENRY JAMES
The Ambassadors, 1903

The gloomy gallery of Notre-Dame.

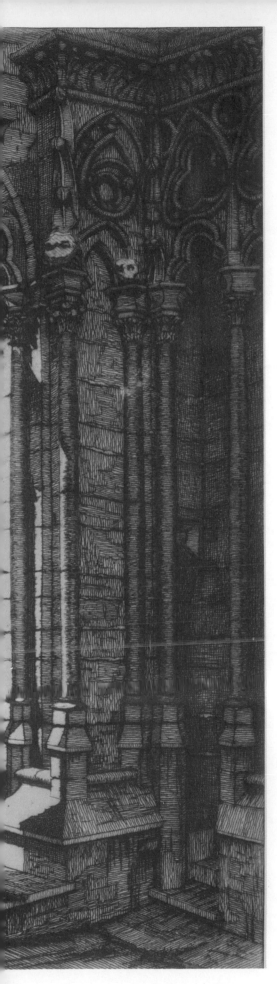

The appeal of Notre-Dame de Paris — a medieval Gothic cathedral devoted to Roman Catholic worship — transcends the limits of time and culture. Kotaro Takamura, a twentieth-century Japanese sculptor and poet, has written a lyrical tribute to France's most famous cathedral.

Another squall!
Looking up at you, the collar of the overcoat
Lifted against the slanting rain — It is I,
He who makes it a rule to come at least once each day —
The Japanese.

This morning
A terrible storm, increasing since daybreak,
Now rages in the four corners of Paris.
I cannot distinguish east from west,
Nor even which way the storm is moving, as it runs amok, here in the
      Ile de France . . .
But here I am again,
Oh Notre-Dame of Paris!
Soaked with rain,
Just to gaze at you, to touch you,
To steal a kiss from you, your flesh of stone. . . .

Oh Notre-Dame, Notre-Dame!
Cathedral like a rock, a mountain, an eagle, a squatting lion —
A hidden rock in a mist,
The bulwark of Paris,
Pelted by blinding rain,
Buffeted head-on by the beating wind,
You rise up before me, oh my Notre-Dame of Paris!
It is I, who look up at you,
The Japanese.
My heart thrills at the sight of you;
Before the semblance of heroic tragedy,
A my youthful heart, come from a strange and different land,
      is over-full —
It throbs irrationally, trembles in time with the screaming air.

Another squall!
How they rage, the four elements, striving to efface you, to turn
      you back to nothingness!
Rain splashes in smoke and phosphorescence;
The scaly spotted cloud grazes against your peaks;
The entwining cyclone seeks to snatch in its claw just one of your belfry
      pillars;
Beyond count, tiny bright fluttering elves collide, burst and stream on
      the tracery of the rose-windows . . .
The gargoyles, glimpsed through the splashes high on the edge of the
      building —
They alone bear the brunt of the fluttering mob of elves,
Lifting their paws and craning their necks,

With bared teeth, voiding the fiery stream of wind and rain . . .
Rows of curious stone saints nod to each other, with odd gestures,
Huge buttresses on the sides lay bare their arms as ever,
And the storm beats on those slanting arcs with all its force!
The peal of the organ on the day of Mass!
What has become of the cock on the thin high steeple?
Fluttering curtains of water are falling on all sides now —
And you stand in the middle of it all. . . .

The rain-beaten Cathedral!
After a pause, another squall, in *allegro* —
Down swings the baton in a sudden flash,
And all the instruments of heaven are in commotion —
All round, the chaotic revolutions of a rhapsody . . .
And in the midst of it, oh Cathedral, towering in sheer silence,
Watching intently over the roofs of storm-ridden Paris!
Do not take it amiss
That someone stands here now,
A hand against your corner-stone,
A fevered cheek against your flesh —
It is I, drunk with beauty,
The Japanese!

KOTARO TAKAMURA
The Rain-beaten Cathedral, 1921

Notre-Dame's location, on the Île de la Cité, heightens its impact.

REFERENCE

Chronology of French History

Entries in boldface refer to Notre-Dame de Paris.

843	Treaty of Verdun divides Charlemagne's empire; Charles the Bald rules a kingdom roughly equivalent in area to modern France
987	Hugh Capet establishes Capetian dynasty
1122	Suger named Abbot of Saint-Denis
1137	Abbot Suger begins rebuilding of abbey of Saint-Denis; Louis VII ascends the throne
1147	Louis VII departs for the Second Crusade; Suger named regent
1160	**Maurice de Sully, new Bishop of Paris, decides to build Notre-Dame de Paris**
1163	**Cornerstone laid; work begun on choir and apse**
1180	Louis VII dies; boy-king Philip Augustus crowned
1182	**Choir and apse completed; papal legate, Henri de Château-Marçay, consecrates high altar**
1185	**Heraclius, Patriarch of Jerusalem, preaches the Third Crusade in new choir**
1196	**Bulk of nave completed; death of Maurice de Sully**
1200	**Western façade begun by new bishop, Eudes de Sully**
1208–13	Albigensian Crusade preached against religious heresy in southern France
1214	Philip Augustus defeats anti-Capetian alliance, led by John of England, at battle of Bouvines
1220	**Western façade completed to level of Gallery of Kings**
c. **1225**	**Rose window of western façade completed**
1225–40	**Southern tower built**
1226	Accession of Louis IX; renewal of the Albigensian Crusade
1229	**Count Raymond of Toulouse, defeated by Albigensian Crusade, does penance in cathedral**
c. **1230**	**Flying buttresses replaced by huge new arches**
1235–40	**Northern tower completed**
c. **1235–45**	**Lateral chapels installed**
1239	**Louis IX brings the Crown of Thorns to Notre-Dame**
1248	Louis IX embarks on the Seventh Crusade
1250	**Towers of western façade and reconstruction of nave completed; work on façade of northern transept begun**
c. 1250	**Northern rose window created**
1258	**Southern transept façade begun by Jean de Chelles**
1259	Treaty of Paris signed; English renounce claims to Normandy and other French provinces
1265–67	**Statues placed above Red Portal**
1270	**Transept façades completed**
1271	**Funeral of Louis IX**
1296–1320	**Chapels of ambulatory built**
1296–1304	Philip the Fair challenges papal supremacy
1297	**Louis IX canonized as Saint Louis; central chapel of apse consecrated in his honor**
1302	First authenticated convocation of Estates General
1304	**Philip the Fair celebrates his victory over the Flemings by riding up nave on horseback**
1309–78	Babylonian Captivity of papacy at Avignon
1318	**Jean Ravy completes flying buttresses and adds chapels to choir**
1338–1453	The Hundred Years' War
1346	French defeated at battle of Crécy
1348–50	The Black Death sweeps across France
1351	**Choir screen completed**
1356	Black Prince defeats French at battle of Poitiers
1358	Peasant uprising in protest against war taxes
1415	Battle of Agincourt; English reconquer Normandy
1418	Dauphin (later Charles VII) flees to southern France
1420	Treaty of Troyes repudiates Dauphin and provides for English succession to the French throne
1422	**Funeral of the mad King Charles VI**
1422–28	Regency of English Duke of Bedford
1429	Joan of Arc lifts English siege of Orléans, making possible the coronation of Charles VII at Reims
1431	Joan of Arc burned at stake by English at Rouen
1431	**Henry VI of England crowned King of France**
1436	Charles VII's troops retake Paris
1456	Posthumous retrial and rehabilitation of Joan of Arc
1515–47	Reign of Francis I
1548	**Huguenots storm Notre-Dame after Council of Trent**

1558	Wedding of Mary Stuart and the Dauphin Francis
1562–98	Religious wars waged against French Huguenots
1572	Henry of Navarre's marriage to Marguerite of Valois the occasion of the massacre of St. Bartholomew's Day
1593	Henry of Navarre abjures Protestantism
1598	Edict of Nantes grants political equality and limited freedom of worship to Huguenots
1610	Accession of Louis XIII
1614	Last meeting of Estates General before Revolution
1625	Marriage of Henrietta Maria of France to King Charles I of England
1631–48	French participation in Thirty Years' War
1638	Louis XIII vows to rebuild main altar; Te Deum chanted at birth of future Louis XIV
1643	Te Deum chanted for coronation of Louis XIV
1648–53	Revolt of the Fronde
1661	Louis XIV assumes absolute personal rule
1675	Funeral of Vicomte de Turenne
1685	Revocation of the Edict of Nantes
1699	Work begun on rebuilding the main altar
1711	Workmen discover remains of Gallo-Roman votive pillars
1713	Treaty of Utrecht confirms permanent separation of crowns of France and Spain
1715	Accession of Louis XV
1726	New roofing installed; northern rose remodeled
1728	Interior of cathedral whitewashed
1741	Stained-glass windows removed
1756–63	Seven Years' War
1771	Soufflot, architect of the Pantheon, enlarges central portal of cathedral
1774	Accession of Louis XVI
1779	Louis XVI and Marie Antoinette organize a mass marriage for 100 poor maidens
1781	Western rose window repaired
1789	Storming of the Bastille; Declaration of the Rights of Man proclaimed
1793	Execution of Louis XVI; beginning of Reign of Terror
1793	Citizens remove statues from the Gallery of Kings
1794	Notre-Dame renamed the Temple of Reason; festival of the Goddess of Reason celebrated
1801	Napoleon signs Concordat with papacy
1802	First Roman Catholic service held since 1793
1804	Napoleon crowns himself emperor at Notre-Dame
1811	Baptism of Napoleon's heir as the King of Rome
1815	Battle of Waterloo
1830	Revolution of 1830; Louis Philippe elected king
1845	Viollet-le-Duc undertakes extensive restorations
1848	Abdication of Louis Philippe; Louis Napoleon named president of the new republic
1852	Coronation of Louis Napoleon as Napoleon III
1853	Marriage of Napoleon III to Spanish Princess Eugénie de Montijo
1864	Restorations completed; cathedral officially reconsecrated in elaborate ceremony
1870–71	Franco-Prussian War; Napoleon III capitulates; Third Republic proclaimed
1871	Notre-Dame set on fire during Paris Commune
1878	Demolition of Hôtel Dieu relieves congestion around cathedral
1894–1906	The Dreyfus Affair
1905	Official separation of Church and State
1909	Beatification of Joan of Arc celebrated
1914–18	World War I
1918	Armistice Te Deum sung
1920	Joan of Arc canonized
1936	First Popular Front ministry under Léon Blum
1939–45	World War II
1940	German forces occupy Paris; fall of France
1944	Liberation of Paris; Te Deum sung in presence of General de Gaulle to celebrate capitulation of German troops
1945–46	De Gaulle serves as interim president
1957	France joins the European Economic Community
1958–59	De Gaulle — recalled during crisis over Algeria — named premier, then president, of Fifth Republic
1963	Restorations of interior undertaken
1968	Cleaning of exterior begun
1969	De Gaulle resigns; Pompidou elected president
1970	State funeral for Charles de Gaulle

Gothic Cathedrals of France

An abiding faith in God, an increase in the wealth of urban centers, and an evolving sophistication of building techniques combined, in the mid-twelfth century, to create a new architectural style that swept rapidly across Europe. Within less than three hundred years, eighty Gothic cathedrals were erected in France alone. Of these, perhaps a dozen stand out from the rest for magnificence and originality.

The new mode — initiated by Abbot Suger in about 1137 at Saint-Denis — inspired an extraordinary surge of dedication and talent as successive bishops and their communities embarked on the Cathedral Crusade. The rebuilt abbey church of Saint-Denis outside Paris formed the prototype of the Gothic. Saint-Denis's emphasis on the transcendental nature of light and the glory of stained glass became the lodestar for innovative advances in size, structure, and ornamentation. The technical devices that were employed in building the great cathedrals — the pointed arch, ribbed vault, and flying buttress — no more define the Gothic than an alphabet defines a language. They were primarily the means by which an aesthetic based on luminosity and verticality could be implemented.

The first Gothic cathedral was built at *Sens*, seventy-five miles southwest of Paris. Under the guidance of Archbishop Henry Sanglier, a friend of Abbot Suger, the original Romanesque plan of 1130 was abandoned in favor of a structure that would incorporate ribbed vaulting throughout. The choir, begun about 1145, was completed in 1163 — the year that ground was broken for Notre-Dame de Paris.

Sens cathedral consists of five main divisions — three square bays in the nave and two in the choir, topped by six-part vaults sprung from pier clusters. The tripartite nave elevation of arcade, triforium, and clerestory may have prompted the advanced design of Chartres

fifty years later. Early in the thirteenth century, the clerestory windows at Sens were enlarged to admit more light, and flying buttresses were installed.

Staunch partisans of Thomas Becket, Henry Sanglier and his successor played host to the exiled English archbishop during his four-year stay at Sens. A vivid stained-glass window in the ambulatory depicts scenes from the martyr's life.

Among the church dignitaries present at the consecration of Saint-Denis in 1144 was Bishop Baudouin II of *Noyon*. Using Suger's choir as a model, he began to rebuild his cathedral in 1150. By 1185 the choir was completed. Work on the nave bays continued until 1205, and the western façade was not finished until 1235. As with other Early Gothic cathedrals, both rounded and pointed arches were used. The original sexpartite vaults of the nave — resting on alternating single and compound pillars — collapsed during a fire in 1293 and were replaced by more conventional quadripartite vaults. Flying buttresses were also added at that time to the nave and choir.

Although the height of Notre-Dame de Noyon is seven feet less than that of Sens, its narrower width contributes to a

greater sense of unbounded spaciousness. The addition of a fourth story to the nave heightens this impression.

The rounded transept arms, built between 1170 and 1185, are the cathedral's most distinctive feature; unfortunately, their magnificent stained-glass windows are no longer in place.

In 1153, three years after ground was broken at Noyon, Bishop Thibaut inaugurated a new cathedral dedicated to the Virgin at *Senlis*. The smallest of French cathedrals — only sixty-nine feet high — it was consecrated in 1191. In the thirteenth century a spire and transept arms were added. In 1504 a severe fire destroyed the upper levels of the choir and transept; as a result, so much of the original structure was rebuilt that only the lovely apse and western façade are examples of pure Early Gothic.

The thirteenth-century architect Villard de Honnecourt declared that the towers of Notre-Dame de *Laon* were the finest he had ever seen. Seven towers were planned but only five were actually built — two on the western façade, one on each transept arm, and a lantern tower above the crossing. The elaborate, traceried western towers are adorned with sixteen carved oxen — said to honor the animals that hauled the building blocks up the steep hill. Succeeding generations echoed Villard's opinion and broadened it to include the entire façade. A masterpiece of comprehensive design, its two levels of porches, gables, turrets, tympana, sculpture, and central rose set the standard for many later cathedrals.

Begun in 1160 by Bishop Gauthier de Montagne, the choir of Laon was completed fourteen years later. By 1190 the transept and five bays of the nave had been erected. In 1205 the final bays of the nave and the western façade were in place. In that year the choir was remodeled, lengthened to encompass ten bays, and given an unusual flat-ended apse. The extreme length of the choir,

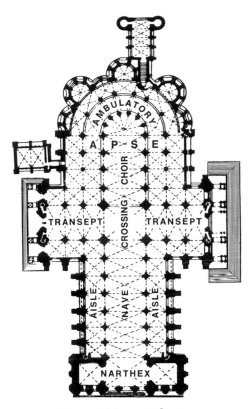

Ground plan of Chartres

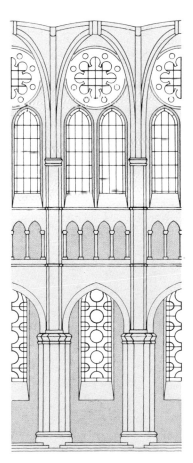

*Chartres's nave elevation:
arcade, triforium, clerestory*

the quadripartite elevation, the seventy-eight-foot-high vaults, and the open lantern tower give the interior of Laon a glowing, airy quality.

Throughout the Middle Ages, the efforts of the cathedral builders were intermittently confounded by the devastating scourge of fire. One such conflagration in 1194 gutted Notre-Dame de *Chartres*; only the Early Gothic crypt built by Bishop Fulbert and the towers, three lancet windows, and the Royal Portal of the western façade survived. The town of Chartres — for centuries the traditional center of the cult of the Virgin —

responded to this disaster by rebuilding its cathedral in the unprecedented span of twenty-seven years.

The unknown master of Chartres synthesized the structural solutions of previous masters to create a new and innovative harmony. For the first time, flying buttresses were designed as an integral part of an entire cathedral. Elimination of the gallery vastly simplified the elevation and made possible the installation of two lancets surmounted by a rose in the forty-five-foot-high clerestory — which matches the height of the nave arcade. The uniform quadripartite vaults — resting on slim piers with four attached colonnettes — are sprung from a point midway in the clerestory and climb to a height 120 feet above the pavement. The plan of the choir, with its double ambulatory and seven radiating chapels of unequal size, was determined by the presence of the old crypt below.

The incomparable stained-glass windows that illuminate the austere interior of Chartres are its main ornament. Chartres alone has retained all of its incredibly beautiful thirteenth-century glass Forty-four feet in diameter, the western rose depicting the Last Judgment is the most famous — but the transept roses and the hundred-odd other windows all contribute to the jewel-like radiance of the cathedral's interior.

The richness of the windows is only rivaled by the abundance of the exterior sculpture. The profusion of 10,000 figures in the triple porches of each transept and in the portals of the western façade is a striking testament to the artistry and genius of the medieval sculptor. Dominating the lofty western façade are the asymmetrical spires of its towers: the severe south steeple, 147 feet high, was completed in the twelfth century; the much taller north spire, built between 1507 and 1513, is a marvel of High Gothic enthusiasm.

The rebuilding of the cathedral of *Bourges* was initiated by Archbishop

Henry de Sully in 1195, the year after Chartres was begun. The choir was finished in 1214, the nave and façade around 1255. Unlike most High Gothic cathedrals, which took their plan from Chartres, Bourges represents a unique departure. By raising the nave arcade — the pier shafts are fifty-four feet high — and reducing the height of the triforium and clerestory, the Bourges master created a church whose lofty proportions are overwhelming. The inner of the two aisles that flank the nave rises to the astounding height of sixty-nine feet — and has its own tripartite elevation. The cathedral shimmers with rainbow-hued light. Bourges' collection of thirteenth-century glass is second only to that of Chartres in quantity and quality.

The massiveness of the cathedral's exterior is accentuated by the absence of a projecting transept. Piercing the broad expanse of the façade are five richly carved portals that exactly reflect the plan of the nave interior.

The plan of the cathedral of *Soissons* shows the unmistakable influence of Chartres. There is the same tripartite elevation, consisting of nearly equal arcade and clerestory levels divided by an arcaded triforium. Begun in 1197, the choir was completed by 1212; the nave by 1225; and the façade by 1250. In the fourteenth century a northern transept arm was added to balance the lovely Early Gothic southern transept, which was built in the 1170's. This charming wing — with its apsidal termination, four-story elevation, and off-center chancel — was miraculously spared during the World War I bombardment that reduced the nave to a near-ruin.

The Romanesque cathedral of *Rouen* was destroyed by fire in 1200; reconstruction along Gothic lines was immediately begun by architect Jean d'Andely. The basic form was completed by 1250 although the southern transept façade was not begun until 1280. Rouen is remarkable for its three beautiful towers and its ornate sixteenth-century façade. Lightning destroyed its central

spire in 1822, and an incongruous cast-iron replacement was installed by 1876. The cathedral suffered serious damage during World War II. In anticipation of the Nazi advance, the outstanding fifteenth-century rose window was removed; the opening is still boarded over.

Notre-Dame de *Reims,* begun in 1210, occupies the site of several earlier cathedrals. As the traditional coronation

site of France's kings, Reims was conceived on a majestic scale. The choir and transept were completed in 1241; the nave and the western façade, to the level of the rose, by 1290. In 1427 — two years before the historic coronation of Charles VII — the last tower of the façade was finally erected.

Although based on the tripartite mode of verticality established at Chartres, Reims has a much longer nave and the inner walls seem even more transparent. Bar tracery appears in the stained-glass windows for the first time. Each column in the sharply pointed nave arcade is adorned with a floral capital that leads the eye effortlessly toward the graceful choir with its single ambulatory and five radiating chapels.

The regal western façade is the stage for five hundred animated figures of saints, angels, kings, and patriarchs. Although severely damaged during World Wars I and II, the cathedral of Reims has been fully restored.

Notre-Dame d'*Amiens* was begun in 1220. Contrary to customary procedure, the nave was completed first, by about 1235. The fire that had consumed the earlier church on the site had spared the old choir; the vaults of the new choir were finally sprung by about 1260.

The largest Gothic cathedral in France, with an area of 9,000 square yards, Amiens is a classic example of High Gothic at its climax. Basing his plan on the Chartrian scheme, Amiens's architect Robert de Luzarches introduced certain modifications appropriate to the huge scale of the cathedral. As at Chartres, the choir consists of four bays flanked by double aisles. Radiating off the single ambulatory are six uniform chapels and one deeper chapel. Wide transept arms stress the Latin cross shape of the cathedral.

The Gothic tendency to "dissolve" the walls of the nave into a multiplicity of window surfaces and soaring lines reaches its peak at Amiens. The sixty-foot-high nave arcade almost equals the combined height of the triforium and clerestory. And the arched arcade of the triforium is linked visually and structurally to the glazed clerestory by a series of slim colonnettes — creating an unbroken line of dramatic ascent.

The imposing façade of Amiens is dominated by the high placement of its sixteenth-century rose window. The massive twin towers that were completed in the late fourteenth century are logically integrated into the whole. Three deep portals, richly carved in relief, correspond to the three aisles of the nave.

Above an open gallery is the traditional array of kings.

Beset by structural problems and natural disasters, the cathedral of *Beauvais* was never completed. The truncated half-church consists of only a choir and transept. The ambitious choir, begun in

1225, was completed in 1272. One hundred and fifty-seven feet above the pavement, the choir vaults are the highest in the world. But in 1284 they collapsed, destroying portions of the choir and apse. Reconstruction proceeded over the next forty years and additional stout piers were installed for increased strength. Work was suspended until the sixteenth century when the transept arms were built. Undaunted by centuries of bad luck, the architects constructed a five-hundred-foot-high openwork spire above the crossing in 1569. Four years later it fell and was never rebuilt.

The unique façade of the cathedral of *Strasbourg* was begun in 1277 and com-

pleted in the mid-fourteenth century. A huge recessed portal is surmounted by two stories of openwork gables and arcades. The northern tower terminates in an awe-inspiring steeple, 466 feet high, that gives the façade a lopsided majesty. Within, the wide and somber nave is adorned with a series of masterful statues of patriarchs and emperors.

Selected Bibliography

Adams, Henry. *Mont Saint-Michel and Chartres*. Boston: Houghton Mifflin Co., 1933.

Bloch, Marc. *Feudal Society*. Translated by L. A. Manyon. 2 vols. Chicago: University of Chicago Press, 1964.

Bottineau, Yves. *Notre-Dame de Paris and the Sainte-Chapelle*. Translated by Lovett F. Edwards. New York: Rand McNally and Co., 1967.

Branner, Robert. *Gothic Architecture*. New York: George Braziller, 1961.

Evans, Joan, ed. *The Flowering of the Middle Ages*. New York: McGraw-Hill Book Co., 1966.

Fletcher, Banister. *A History of Architecture*. 17th ed., rev. New York: Charles Scribner's Sons, 1967.

Frankl, Paul. *The Gothic*. Princeton: Princeton University Press, 1960.

Gimpel, Jean. *The Cathedral Builders*. New York: Grove Press, 1961.

Jantzen, Hans. *High Gothic*. Translated by James Palmer. New York: Pantheon Books, 1962.

Postgate, R. W. *Revolution from 1789 to 1906*. New York: Harper & Row, 1962.

Roubier, Jean. *Notre-Dame de Paris*. Paris: M.-J. Challamel, 1954.

Simson, Otto von. *The Gothic Cathedral*. New York: Pantheon Books, 1956.

Stoddard, Whitney S. *Monastery and Cathedral in France*. Middletown, Conn.: Wesleyan University Press, 1966.

Temko, Allan. *Notre-Dame of Paris*. New York: The Viking Press, 1959.

Acknowledgments and Picture Credits

The Editors make grateful acknowledgment for the use of excerpted material from the following works:

Cathedrals of France by Auguste Rodin. Translated by Elizabeth Chase Geissbuhler. Copyright 1965 by Elizabeth Chase Geissbuhler. The excerpt appearing on pages 141-42 is reproduced by permission of Beacon Press and Hamlyn Publishing Group Ltd.

Gargantua and Pantagruel by François Rabelais. The extract on pages 151-52 is from The Heritage Press edition, translated by Jacques LeClercq, reproduced by permission of The George Macy Companies, Inc., copyright 1936, renewed 1964.

Paris by Hilaire Belloc. Copyright 1902 by Methuen & Co. Ltd. The excerpt appearing on pages 139-41 is reproduced by permission of A. D. Peters & Co.

Parisian Points of View by Ludovic Halévy. The quotation from the novel appears on page 127. New York: Harper and Brothers, 1894.

"The Rain-beaten Cathedral" by Kotaro Takamura. The selection appearing on pages 159-60 is reproduced by permission of John Murray Ltd.

The Editors would like to express their particular appreciation to the Musée Notre-Dame in Paris for its generous cooperation, to Robert Branner of Columbia University for his critical comments on the text, to Kate Lewin in Paris for her invaluable assistance in obtaining pictorial material, and to Adam Woolfitt in London for his creative photography. In addition the Editors would like to thank the following organizations and individuals:

Centre de Recherches sur les Monuments Historiques — Mme. Legendre
Marilyn Flaig, New York
Pierre Joly — Musée Notre-Dame

The title or description of each picture appears after the page number (boldface), followed by its location. Photographic credits appear in parentheses. The following abbreviations are used:

AN,P	— Archives Nationales, Paris	BL	— Boudot-Lamotte
AP,P	— Archives Photographiques, Paris	MMA	— Metropolitan Museum of Art
BN,P	— Bibliothèque Nationale, Paris	MND(D)	— Musée Notre-Dame (Dorka)

ENDPAPERS Anonymous colored engraving of Notre-Dame, 19th century. Musée Carnavalet (Dorka) HALF TITLE Symbol designed by Jay J. Smith Studio FRONTISPIECE Exterior of southeast side of the apse (Adam Woolfitt) **9** Silver and gilded copper reliquary of the right arm of St. Louis, 14th century. Château de Castelnau-de-Bretenoux, Prudhomat (Dorka) **10** Engraving of the western façade with superimposed spires, from *Discourses on Architecture* by Eugène Emmanuel Viollet-le-Duc, 1889 **12-13** Illumination of Louis II, Duke of Anjou, arriving in Paris, from *Chroniques de Froissart de Louis Bruges*. BN,P, Ms. Fr. 2645, fol 321v

CHAPTER I **14** Gargoyles on the tower (Culver Pictures) **16-17** Notre-Dame from the south at dawn (Adam Woolfitt) **18-19** Three reliefs from a Gallo-Roman votive pillar. Musée de Cluny **20** Illumination of St. Denis preaching in Paris, from *La Vie de Mgr. St. Denis*, 14th century. BN,P, Ms. Fr. 2091, fol 111 **21** Statue of St. Denis, from the Portal of the Virgin (Adam Woolfitt)

preaching, 16th century. British Museum, Ms. Add. 4727, fol 2; right, Engraving of rioters in a church, from *Engravings of Scenes from the History of France and the Netherlands* by Franz Hogenberg, 1559–82. Spencer Collection, New York Public Library **95** Detail of an anonymous painting of *The Field of the Cloth of Gold,* 16th century. Her Majesty the Queen. Copyright Reserved **96** Medal commemorating the marriage of Francis II and Mary Stuart by Guillaume Martin, 1558. MMA, Anonymous Gift, 1907 **98** Painting of the *Massacre of the Innocents* by François Dubois, 16th century. Musée Cantonal des Beaux Arts, Lausanne (André Held) **99** Engraving of Henry IV entering Paris by Leclerc after Bollery. BN,P **100** left, Engraving of the second of the three miracles of the Virgin, 1626. Collection Joly (Dorka); right, Engraving of the Te Deum for the victory at Avain, 1635. BN,P **101** Drawing of the arrival at Notre-Dame of the flags taken at Rhinfeld, 1638. Cabinet des Estampes, BN,P **102** Interior of Notre-Dame showing the elevation (Adam Woolfitt) **103** Medal commemorating the Declaration of St. Germain, February 10, 1638, by I. Bernard. Collection Joly (Dorka)

CHAPTER VI **105** Gargoyles on the tower (Adam Woolfitt) **106** top, Marble statue of Louis XIII in Notre-Dame; bottom, Marble statue of Louis XIV in Notre-Dame; both by Antoine Coysevox (both, Adam Wollfitt) **107** left, Pen drawing of the major altar of Louis XIII by Jules Hardouin-Mansard, 1699. AN,P (Dorka); right, Anonymous painting of north crosspiece of Notre-Dame at the end of the 18th century. MND(D) **108** left, Engraving of the southern rose window by Aveline, 1727. MND (D); right, Watercolor of a high window of the nave by Pierre and Jean le Vieil, 1756. AN,P (Dorka) **109** Engraving of the funeral of Philip V, King of Spain, by C. N. Cochin, 1746. MND (D) **110-11** Engraving of the reception of Marie Antoinette at Notre-Dame after the birth of Louis Joseph Xavier François by Née after Moitte, 1782. MND (D) **112** Engraving of the confession of Favras before Notre-Dame by Berthault, 1790. Musée Carnavalet, Paris (Dorka) **113** Engraving of the taking of the Bastille by Janinet, 1789. Collection Roger Castaing (Dorka) **114** left, Engraving of Louis XVI and his family in the prison garden (Bulloz); right, Engraving of the beheading of Louis XVI, from *La Revolution Française* by Berthault, 1793. Cabinet des Estampes, BN,P **115** Sketch of Marie Antoinette by Jacques Louis David, 1793. Louvre (Bulloz) **117** Engraving of the entrance of First Consul Napoleon Bonaparte to Notre-Dame, Easter 1802. Collection Roger Castaing (Dorka) **118** Medal of Napoleon by David d'Angers. MMA, Rogers Fund, 1908 **119** top and bottom, Preliminary sketches of Napoleon and Joséphine for *Le Sacre* by Jacques Louis David, 1805-7. Louvre (Bulloz) **120-21** *Le Sacre,* by Jacques Louis David, 1805–7. Louvre

CHAPTER VII **123** Gargoyles on the tower (Culver Pictures) **124** left, Sketch of the sack of the archiepiscopal palace by Viollet-le-Duc, 1831; right, Portrait of Viollet-le-Duc by Monvoison, 1834. AP,P **125** Watercolor of the demolition around Notre-Dame, 19th century. Collection Joly (Dorka) **126** Watercolor of the reliquary for the Crown of Thorns by Viollet-le-Duc. AP,P **127** Sketch of the choir grilles by Viollet-le-Duc. AP,P **128** The spire by Viollet-le-Duc, 1860 (Adam Woolfitt) **129** The portals of the western façade sandbagged in 1918 (Roger Viollet) **130** The towers from the southeast (Adam Woolfitt) **131** The buttresses from the roof (Adam Woolfitt) **132** De Gaulle and Leclerc at Notre-Dame, August 26, 1944. MND (L.A.P.I.) **135** Notre-Dame at twilight from the east. (Adam Woolfitt)

NOTRE-DAME IN LITERATURE **136** Statue of St. Thomas with the features of Viollet-le-Duc on the spire at Notre-Dame by Geoffroy-Dechaume (Adam Woolfitt) **139** Drawing of the buttress of the tower by Viollet-le-Duc. BL **140-41** Three sketches of church architecture by Auguste Rodin, 1914 (New York Public Library) **142-43** Anonymous engraving of a procession for Sainte Geneviève, 1652. BN,P(D) **144-45** Engraving of a procession for Sainte Geneviève by Blanchard, 1693. BN,P(D) **146-47** Anonymous engraving of the Archbishop of Paris blessing the faithful, 1865. *Monde Illustré,* April 22, 1865 (Dorka) **148-49** Engraving of the consecration at Notre-Dame by F. Thorigay, from *Monde Illustré,* June 11, 1864. BN,P (D) **150** Engraving of Gargantua by Gustave Doré, from *Gargantua* by François Rabelais (The Granger Collection) **152-53** Engraving from Victor Hugo's *Notre-Dame de Paris,* 1882 (Dorka) **154** Engraving of a gargoyle overlooking Paris by Charles Meryon. MMA, H.O. Havemeyer Collection, 1929 **155** Engraving by Steinheil Laisne from Victor Hugo's *Notre-Dame de Paris* (Dorka) **156-57** Engraving of the western façade, from *Collection de Vues de Paris,* 1845-51. George Eastman House **158-59** Engraving of the gallery by Charles Meryon. MMA, Harris Brisbane Dick Fund, 1917 **160** Engraving of Notre-Dame and the île de la Cité by Charles Meryon. MMA, H.O. Havemeyer Collection, 1929

REFERENCE **164** The nave of the cathedral of Sens. BL **165** top left, The cathedral of Laon (French Government Tourist Office); bottom left, The Royal Portal at the cathedral of Chartres. BL; top and bottom right, drawings by Francis & Shaw, Inc. **166** left, The elevation at the cathedral of Bourges; center, The cathedral of Rouen. Both, BL; right, The western rose window at the cathedral of Reims (French Government Tourist Office) **167** top center, The cathedral of Amiens (French Government Tourist Office); bottom center, The cathedral of Beauvais from the air (Alain Perceval); right, The cathedral of Strasbourg (French Government Tourist Office)

Index